A CHANGE OF HEART

Realigning Your Life to
Unlock Your True Potential

What people are saying about *A Change of Heart*:

Gerdi van den Berg is someone who understands God's heartbeat and the ways in which He leads people to change ... if they let Him. Her scientific background and the spiritual insight that she uses to lead people to change comprehensively are her strongest gifts ... I believe God will use *A Change of Heart* to lead you to permanent, holistic change, and that your understanding of God and his role in each of your life's dimensions will only deepen.

– Marius Malan,
pastor at Kompas Church, Vanderbijlpark

I am privileged to call Gerdi my 'Capetonian mom'. I cannot quantify the amount of wisdom, advice, and encouragement I have received from, and the laughter I have shared with, this formidable Proverbs 31 woman. Her book offers answers to everyday questions and practical guidelines that many people long for and search for, usually in vain. Here you will find answers to 'If only I ...' groans and 'Why don't I find fulfilment?' questions.

– Leandie du Randt,
actress, writer, and motivational speaker

When drought devastates our heartscapes, it becomes difficult to hear God's love song in our inner being and to take control of our lives. Gerdi reminds us that God promised us re-creating care. In this Spirit-filled book she shows us how our attitude towards ourselves and others can be renewed, and how Jesus can bless us with flexibility, so that we can live a fulfilling, victorious life.

– Elize Parker,
journalist and novelist

In *A Change of Heart*, Gerdi shares divine truths that she has discovered along the way – often at greater cost to herself than people realise. In this book she succeeds in expressing the way that I, too, understand our divine purpose and the importance of identity and relationships in a fresh and novel manner.

– Hein Vorster,
psychologist and pastor at Powerhouse
Ministries International, Durbanville

Gerdi van den Berg is a gifted counsellor on a mission to help people change and find their joy. In this carefully structured book, she invites you to step into your wholeness. The real-life stories are sensitively curated, relatable, and engaging, reflecting her knowledge and years of experience.

A Change of Heart is also an invaluable resource for those who seek to develop their skills as counsellors. We strongly commend it to every person who seeks meaningful growth.

– BRUCE AND JUDY MCCALLUM,
SENIOR PASTORS, EL SHADDAI CHRISTIAN CHURCH,
DURBANVILLE

A CHANGE OF HEART

Realigning Your Life to
Unlock Your True Potential

DR GERDI VAN DEN BERG

GLOBAL
PUBLISHING

A CHANGE OF HEART

Published by Global Publishing, an imprint of Global Publishing Partners, LLC
Nashville, TN, USA

This edition © 2024
First edition 2023
Text © Gerdi van den Berg 2023

Cover design, layout and DTP by De Wet van Deventer
Author photo by Brenda Veldtman
Images sourced from Freepik.com

ISBN 979-8-89317-100-6

CONTENTS

PART 3 – HOW WE CHANGE

CHAPTER 10: Harmony

CHAPTER 11: Change

CHAPTER 12: Maintenance

ACKNOWLEDGEMENTS

would like to thank my husband for his ongoing encouragement and support. Cobus often displays the fruit of re-creation in his endeavours.

Thank you also to each of my children. Lorraine, for your particular enthusiasm and encouragement during the writing of this book. Thank you for taking care of my backup copies. Christiaan, Daniela, Llewellyn, Johan and Leandie for your sincere love and care. I feel very privileged to be your friend and to walk alongside you on life's journey. I am so grateful that we can share the whole of eternity. Thank you to my mentors and sisters in Christ. Elize Parker, your wisdom and patience with me is an invaluable gift. Thea Brink, your editing of the original manuscript sharpened and polished my words so that the message could flow more freely. I have enormous appreciation and respect for the care with which you wielded your expertise. My gratitude and appreciation also go to Hanlie de Lange, Estelle Beyers and Elmie Venter for your loving support and for being my prayer warriors to give this message wings. You celebrate my heart.

Thank you, Francois Griebenow, for reshaping my Afrikaans text into a version I am very proud of. Your gift to recognise the intent of the text is admirable. I appreciate the time and expertise you invested in *A Change of Heart*.

Thank you to every client who has enriched my life, and to those who still do. You are brave and your stamina to confront life issues is admirable. I salute everyone who has walked into my consulting room in the past 25 years.

HOW TO READ THIS BOOK

The aim of this book is to help you unlock long-term change, whether in yourself or in someone you are helping. Too many people are caught up in life-limiting habits and past hurt when they can enjoy healthy relationships, wholeness and a life where all their constituent parts are correctly aligned.

As such, the book will be helpful to individuals who want to tackle issues they struggle with, small groups who gather for Bible study or fellowship, ministry students, as well as Christian psychologists and counsellors. The book will help 'ordinary' believers as well as profession-al Christian practitioners to discern practical steps to effect transforma-tion. The role of groups in bringing about change in counselees, church members and friends should also not be underestimated. (That is why I often work with groups.) To that end, each chapter ends with discussion questions that can aid reflection, benchmarking, and realignment.

The book consists of three parts:

- Part 1, How We Live, shares six ways in which our lives often go pear-shaped, as well as our misguided efforts to rectify that. The chapters stand alone and can be read in any order. Maybe you have taken some of these detours and tried to get back on track with an 'if only': if only my past was different or if only my circumstances would change. No doubt this proved to be a waste of your time and energy, leaving you disappointed and even desperate. Whatever the case may be, you may recognise yourself in some of the case studies and find hope in the change these people experienced.
- Part 2, Who We Are, builds a solid foundation for long-term change. To truly know ourselves is one of our core quests. It is also the key to understanding our behaviour – the big choices as well as the small, everyday ones. The chapters on identity, composition and cooperation disclose our origins, the reason we exist and our constituent parts. This

is required reading and should be tackled chronologically. It is fine to start with Part 2 and refer to Part 1, when necessary, but you cannot skip to Part 3, How We Change, before you have read Part 2.

- Part 3, How We Change, builds on the foundation laid in Part 2. It presents the reader with practical steps to follow on the road to truth and wholeness that manifest in behaviour. These chapters, too, should be read in the order they appear. It is important to work through this content in an attentive and prayerful manner, and to actively incorporate the principles that are discussed. The result will be a life that is properly aligned and governed by true convictions that bring peace, joy, and wisdom.

'Truth' is a concept that is often mentioned in this book. Please note that, when I talk about 'your truth' or 'my truth', I do not mean that all truths are created equal. There is such a thing as absolute truth. He is a Person. True transformation is only possible to the extent in which we align the aspects of our being to Jesus Christ as He is revealed in the Bible.

My life philosophy is also based on the Bible, for which I offer no apology. Having said that, I am a fellow traveller on the journey of life who offers advice based on my experience and interpretation. I encourage you to read this book with an open mind and to accompany me in the search for God's truth. We will need eternity to fully fathom it.

The case studies mentioned in this book represent situations I have encountered over many years in my counselling practice. No one story belongs to a specific person. I use the stories to communicate certain principles while respecting my clients' right to privacy. All names have been changed.

I invite you to journey with me on this quest to align your personal convictions and the aspects of your being with ultimate life-giving truth. I trust that you will get to know your true identity, and that it will motivate you to live a life where the harmony in your inner being spills over into your environment.

May we change for our own good and for God's glory!

FOREWORD

Redemption, reconciliation, and restoration are key actions in the work of the Father, Jesus Christ and the Holy Spirit. Each person in the Holy Trinity fulfils his role in the realignment of humans to the position they held before the Fall. They work continuously, holistically, and in harmony with each other. The Holy Spirit never leaves a person. Romans 8:14 states: 'For those who are led by the Spirit of God are the children of God' (NIV).

In *A Change of Heart*, Gerdi utilises her understanding and years of counselling experience to write an insightful and practical book about our need as humans to be restored to our former position. Her concept of 'realignment' accurately describes the process we need to embark on to achieve this.

In this very practical book, Gerdi investigates the substitute saviours such as lifestyle, diet and positive thinking that we employ to deal with trauma or dissatisfaction. She then goes on to discuss how God has knit us together, and how we can use that knowledge in our quest for lasting change.

In *A Change of Heart*, the issues of the past come under the searchlight. Opening the door to the past might be a challenge, but leads to a deeper understanding of generational struggles and how to overcome them. Even though we are influenced by previous generations, Gerdi makes it clear that we are not stuck in the past and that we should focus on a realigned future.

She emphasises the importance of taking ownership and actively co-operating with the Holy Spirit if we are to work out our redemption and change for the better. Wrong assumptions only make us go in circles. Mistaken beliefs about the self, the world, and God call for realignment. Gerdi includes practical advice about how to rectify fruitless efforts that lead to disappointment. She shows how deep change only occurs when it has an eternal quality and explains several key concepts that need to be addressed to achieve that.

This is truly a valuable book for every person who seeks change, inner harmony, and a life of victory.

– Nicolene Joubert (PhD)
Founder and MD of the Institute
of Christian Psychology (www.icp.org.za)
Professor of Psychology and Christian Counselling
at Houston Christian University, Texas, USA

INTRODUCTION

A few days ago, I ran into a friend of mine at the shop. While catching up, I realised just how temporary change often is. People try to change their lives, but it only lasts for a while. It adds to their frustration and challenges their faith repeatedly, until we simply stop believing that change is even possible. We become cynical and bitter or even, like my friend, deeply depressed.

My clients often tell me, despondently, about years of effort without a significant breakthrough. They doubt the possibility of change, especially since their previous attempts had been in vain.

Is change possible?

> **Sustainable renewal only comes through the penetration and confirmation of God's truth at a heart-level.**

It certainly is. In fact, it is not just possible, it is non-negotiable. However, change only occurs if it has an eternal quality. Permanent change that has eternal value only becomes possible when renewal penetrates to the very core of our being. Such a change results in total transformation, a denial of our own interpretations and assumptions, and discovery and acceptance of God's truth.

People are created to be in a relationship with the Creator God, and to worship Him in spirit and in truth. That requires us to know the Spirit and the truth. We can only have a deep and meaningful relationship with God when we know the truth about our identity, other people, and Him.

Our life experiences play a huge role in how our truth is formed. Our personal truth, the truth as we perceive it, is in charge of our entire being: what we think, what we choose and how we react. It manages our perceptions and our opinions. It determines our attitude towards life. However, the question remains: 'Is our truth God's truth?' Ideally, when we become aware that some of our daily experiences do not echo God's truth as it is revealed in his Word, we start searching for renewal and change.

How is it that our truth so often clashes with his? And why is mere reading of his Word and the knowledge we gain by doing so not enough to bring about much needed change? It is my prayer that, by the end of the book, you will have answers to both these questions. It will require re-creation, a radical about-face of your personal, human interpretations and assumptions to embrace God's revelation.

There are certain requirements for effective renewal. Our being is not divided into separate, independent components; each part of us is interdependent on the others. There is constant non-verbal communication between the different aspects of our being. How we listen to it and the extent to which our inner language becomes discernible to us are very important. In ourselves we have a core, the deepest part of our inner being. It is here where our deepest decision-making takes place. If we want to assert ourselves, we should know this core and bring it in line with the rest of what we know about our make-up. It is almost like gutter pipes that fit into each other to channel the flow of water to the desired destination. In our case, the destination is uninterrupted unity with our Creator and Re-Creator, the only place where we can experience transcendent peace and eternal joy. Without it, we are stuck with a subsistence approach to life.

This book was written to equip and enable you to experience sustainable change. When change comes through truth and lasts, true re-creation has taken place.

Realignment is a requirement for re-creation.

The processing of information that becomes apparent during cognitive behavioural therapy is interwoven with the re-creation process, i.e. the changing of our entire being. Cognitive therapy helps people to see their perceptions and convictions for what they are: not necessarily the truth. It also helps them to change those perceptions so that they can function more effectively. Your modes of thinking, knowledge, understanding and the behavioural choices that stem from your perceptions are employed to change your thought patterns and conform to your new heart convictions. A sound understanding of the principles of cognitive neuroscience goes a long way towards providing insight into the process of change.

Inner order is needed before people can function effectively and experience the fullness of a life-giving relationship with God. To create that inner order and experience God's re-creation, realignment[1] needs to happen. The better you understand this inner order, the more prepared you are to do the work to establish it so that you can be realigned and experience the necessary change. Sustainable renewal only comes through the penetration and confirmation of God's truth at a heart-level. Realignment is a requirement for re-creation.

---

1. The dictionary meaning of 'realignment' may differ slightly from the meaning intended in this book. Here it refers to the requirement that the heart should be 'brought into line' with a new set of truths and assumptions, much like the wheels on a car need to be realigned to run properly.

PART 1

HOW WE LIVE

Assumptions that will
keep you going in circles

f. That short word that indicates a condition. Not when, but if. Almost as if the word itself indicates an unlikely chance, something you have no control over. You are fenced in. Exposed. Powerless.

Or are you? 'If' can indicate something unlikely or it can indicate hope. 'If I ...' can point the way out of bad situations and equip you to take the right steps to a life of abundance. It can motivate you to execute those steps one by one. Surefootedly. Focused and excited. The conditionality of such an 'if' is therefore brimming with energy and momentum – a 'Watch out, world, here I come!' momentum.

However, the opposite is also true. Your thoughts about your prospective course of action can also trap you in an unhealthy and unhappy situation. The things you think you should do to improve your situation lead to the opposite outcome. Instead of accelerating your growth, they act as a handbrake.

There are quite a few of these conditions or things you think you ought to do that can lead you down the wrong track. Sometimes society called out 'if' on your behalf. You were made to understand that nothing would change before some or other condition was met. You *believe* society. You *believe* your environment. You *believe* your past. You *believe* your culture. You grant it top priority in your decision-making and in your definition of yourself.

You do what society and your culture and your peers tell you to. Still, you do not manage to change your situation.

Does that mean that you are done for? Are you doomed to stay where you are? Not at all. However, it does mean that you must subject the conditions you impose upon yourself to serious scrutiny. You should compare your 'ifs' to God's truth. Only then will you be able to strike out in a new, liberating direction. You will gain courage and start living with hope. When you start applying God's truth in your life, you become receptive to fresh knowledge and insight. You can reach the destination God intended for you, the one He created you for.

Before we can set out on the road of truth and hope, we need to make sure we can discern the detours that will delay our progress. In the six chapters of Part 1, we will discuss a few common detours. There are very few people on earth who do not end up on one of them at some stage of their lives.

CHAPTER 1

RELIGION

If only I … prayed more and **knew more Bible verses**

When you fill a two-litre bottle from a tap, you can never fill it beyond its designated capacity. Once it is full, you can fill all you want, but the excess water will go to waste. The volume of the bottle remains two litres, despite your best efforts to exceed it. The bottle's size sets its limit. The source might have lots more to give, but it is the receptacle's capacity that determines how much is received.

Like the bottle, every person's capacity for receiving has a limit, albeit less visible. Even when we're connected to God's inexhaustible reservoir of truth, our inner capacity to receive it will be limited. The amount of truth we can receive from the free-flowing tap of God's Word depends on this limit, the level of our inner capacity. We are limited.

> **God's light and healing power can find their way into our hearts.**

But we would like to receive more of our Heavenly Father's truth. We want to integrate it into our lives. We would love to drink much more from this life source. Every day. And we would like to keep it, assimilate it. How can we grow our capacity?

The piercing Word

In Hebrews 4:12 we read the following: 'For the word of God is living and powerful, and sharper than any two-edged sword, piercing even to the division of soul and spirit, and of joints and marrow, and is a discerner of the thoughts and intents of the heart.' Two truths immediately present themselves: the Word of God cuts, and something is being cut.

That something is a someone – us. We are the object being pierced and penetrated by the Word, sometimes knowingly and often unknowingly. It exposes our inner world and blazes a trail for change. In verses 13 to 15, the author highlights the futility of trying to hide anything from the living God. God sees all and knows how to expose it in such a way that his light and healing power can find their way into our hearts. The passage also reminds us that Jesus is our High Priest, who intercedes for us and who understands our weaknesses. He does on our behalf what we could not do for ourselves.

Where none seems possible, He makes a way – one that offers hope and freedom, but more importantly, eternity with Him, our Saviour and Intercessor.

This remains one of the key aspects that precede lasting change: Who Jesus is for me. We can only feel safe and secure with Him when we get to know Him as our Saviour and Intercessor. We must feel safe before our inner capacity will expand. If we do not feel safe, the doors to our inner world remain shut and we post heavily armed sentinels to guard our secret repositories. These sentinels are Fear, Guilt, and Shame, and their relief guard consists of Anger, Bitterness, Stubbornness, and Hate. They never desert their post and their swords, Limitation and Confusion, are menacingly crossed in front of the black gates.

Maybe we should begin by asking: Why is it so difficult to allow the Word to pierce and expose our inner lives? Why do we rail against something so pure and edifying?

Maybe you simply feel unable to allow a holy God anywhere near your shame. Maybe you feel so insecure that all your defence mechanisms kick in. You would rather endure the agony than risk exposure.

Exposure necessitates confrontation. When you open up, light shines on the deep, dark places that you have worked so hard to conceal for so long. How many times you have wished that these dark secrets would disappear! You have tried every trick to banish them, including rationalisation and denial. If only! The stigma taunts you while it lounges comfortably in your inner recesses. After all, you invited and even welcomed the cover-ups.

As long as your shameful secrets make you feel rejected or humiliated, opening up is not an option. You are convinced that important people in your life will shun you, which would feel like a deathblow.

Many ways to minister the Word

Words are creative. They create atmosphere, friendships, enmity, purpose, and confusion. Words can have minor or major consequences. Words influence the people who hear them. Their impact depends on the source and the platform. Words hide different types of energy that act like invisible attachments, exploding in the receiver's inner world, either enhancing or poisoning it.

> **God's power, wisdom, and goodness**
> **are always intertwined.**

All words can cut, but the Word of God does so in a unique way. A double-edged blade can be used for good or bad. It can either renew, liberate, and heal, or it can wound, paralyse, and even kill. Several factors determine how application of this blade works out for you.

The Word can speak to us one-on-one, raw and direct, although we mostly read or listen to it through filters we have developed. We hear it in a certain way. When we approach the Word primarily through our inner devastation, the filter of our pain can distort its interpretation dramatically.

The Word might also come to us through someone else, who adds their own motivations, energy, and understanding to it. It is possible for the double-edged blade of the Word to trap us in a corner or even hurt us, if it is not applied in an edifying, judicious manner. This often happens when people with the best intentions rush in where angels fear to tread, Bible firmly tucked beneath the arm.

Colossians 1:4 tells of Paul's gratitude about the fellowship's faith. *The Amplified Bible* gives the following definition of faith: "The leaning of your entire human personality on Him in absolute trust and confidence in His power, wisdom, and goodness." The believers in Colosse leaned on Jesus with this kind of trust and confidence. God's power, wisdom, and goodness are always intertwined, a divine threefold cord that cannot be divided into its separate parts. The attributes of God mentioned in this verse happen to form the framework for any successful ministry from God's Word. Every minister of the Word needs to incorporate these attributes when sharing the Word with others. When the divine threefold cord is used, God's Word cuts cleanly and accurately. It pulls the person who is being ministered to from the deepest pit. It points the way to hope and leads to peace.

When any of these three components is omitted, the truth of the Word is distorted. That is when the blade goes askew, hurting instead of healing. A heavy, unnecessary burden is placed on the recipient's shoulders – shoulders which are likely carrying some weighty matters already. When someone proclaims the Word without wisdom, it can do more harm than good, even if it is done in kindness and with the best intentions. When someone uses the Word to manipulate others into specific actions or decisions, that is tantamount to spiritual abuse. I would even go so far to call it charismatic witchcraft.

If any strand of the threefold cord (power, wisdom, and goodness) is missing from the ministry of the Word, damage ensues. Power that lacks wisdom and goodness is harmful. On the other hand, without power, goodness and wisdom are not nearly as effective as their intentions would have them be. Power and wisdom without goodness could come across as cold and clinical. Power and goodness without wisdom can wreak great havoc. Ministry of the Word that lacks wisdom will tear down, destroy, and confuse. Almost always, it leads to judgement, even though the goal is to 'encourage' or to 'admonish'. Sadly, this type of 'ministry of the Word' has led to thousands upon thousands of walking wounded.

One of them ended up in my consulting room one day. His story represents many people who either suffer in silence, or eventually become despondent and quit their faith because it 'doesn't work for them'. They feel they are simply too sinful.

Michael

'We feel the Lord is saying you need to trust in his Word more, Michael.'

Geoff eyes Michael warily. Sure, he does not want to scare off the new guy, but he should at least make the group's feelings clear. Or at least the three of them who discussed Michael's crisis during their coffee break.

Some of the others are still reeling after Michael's confession earlier. They expected more from him! Melody sent running commentary to her WhatsApp group as they were discussing it. Such a big issue warrants prayer, after all ...

After coffee, the group takes prayer requests, as usual. The members take turns to stand in the middle of the circle, while the rest of the group prays or counsels as they feel led. Soon it is Michael's turn. The only Scripture he can think of is Hosea 10:8: 'Then they will say to the mountains, "Cover us!" and to the hills, "Fall on us!"' There was a reason why he had waited three whole months before sharing his struggle. He was afraid that they would react like this. But who knows? Maybe they are right.

'My spirit witnesses with what Geoff said, Michael.'

Stuart stands squarely in front of Michael with his hand on his shoulder. As the group leader, he is the one who encouraged Michael to share his issue with the group.

'In 1 Timothy 4:12 the Lord says that we should be an example to others in word, in conduct, in love, in spirit, in faith, and ...' He pauses to make sure that he has Michael's undivided attention: 'And in purity.'

Stuart clears his throat. Sometimes it is really challenging to be group leader, but he can't let Michael off the hook. Everybody is looking to him for guidance. If he messes this up, they will think that he has feet of clay. Or worse, that he is guilty of the same. He feels for Michael, but good heavens! The guy can't just drop a bomb like that and expect the group to handle him with kid gloves! Besides, he knows several guys who can do with this Scripture, so he pushes through. They are done praying, but Stuart isn't done talking. He embellishes on the verse he quoted and feels quite chuffed that he could think of such an apt Scripture on the spot.

At last, Michael gets to sit down. His body and mind feel numb. In his head a voice is shouting: 'I knew it! I should have kept my trap shut! My goodness, Michael, when will you learn? Nobody will ever understand! Nobody. What happens now, Lord? What am I to do?'

With Stuart on a roll, Michael evaluates his options. Maybe if he adds more Scripture verses about victorious living to the ones on the fridge and memorise them … Maybe if he increased the time he spends on devotions …

And yet, Michael will put most of his Christian brothers and sisters to shame when it comes to quoting Scripture. He has a verse for every situation and 'stands on Scripture' as if his life depended on it. In fact, to him it does. He is convinced that the mature Christians would reject him outright if they had any idea what his heart looked like. Maybe God would too.

A stubborn monster

Michael gingerly walked into my office. The dark mantle of shame hung almost visibly around his shoulders. He was very dejected and depressed.

'Will you tell me why you came, Michael?' I asked.

Once he had gained some momentum, the words came tumbling out. His inner capacity for self-acceptance was severely limited. Maybe it could be attributed to those Scriptures he was so fond of quoting.

'I don't get it! I'm doing everything I possibly can, but this monster won't let me be!'

With his face in his hands, he sobbed out his misery.

'I'm the worst Christian ever. Every day I disappoint God. How can God forgive my sins – especially if I keep on repeating them? I'm sure He does an eyeroll every time I start praying: "Lord, forgive me, I did it again …"'

I put a paper tissue on his knee.

'I don't think so,' I said. 'The God I serve never does an eyeroll when one of his children invites Him into their struggle.'

Michael's monster was pornography. It had grabbed hold of his heart when he was repeatedly sexually abused as a young boy, and now those memories were holding him captive. This monster does not like to let go, especially if it manages to catch its prey at a tender age. Sexual abuse affects the deepest recesses of a boy's (or a girl's) being. It shifts and distorts the child's self-image and leaves the young victim in terrible turmoil. When a child is forced to do things that make them uncomfortable, alarm bells go off in their heads. The underage victim knows these acts are not right. However, the right to say 'no' is cruelly stripped away. This leaves the child dazed and fearful, but at the same time extremely angry. To add insult to injury, he or she has to figure out how to go on with life in such a way that nobody suspects that anything's amiss. 'After all, it's my sin and my shame, not so?' the child reasons.

Abused children often believe that they played a part in the evil that was perpetrated on them, especially if they failed to ask for help. This is what happened to Michael. His uncle spoiled him with sweets and the flashiest skateboards. However, after every abusive incident the same 'nice' uncle also assured him that he, Michael, was the guilty one, and that no one would believe him if he came forward. Keeping their secret kept both of them safe, his mother's brother would say. If Michael blabbed, they might take him from his mom. They would say that his mom is unfit to look after her son if she did not even know what he was doing behind closed doors. Michael should just keep his mouth shut.

> ## Addiction commands an army of obedient, fearful, misguided slaves.

Michael did speak out, but in all the wrong ways – ways that kept his inner story hidden, leading him and those who wanted to help him astray, and leaving his inner world in a tangled, painful mess.

'Michael,' I said, 'who would you like to be?'

'I want to be free, free of this torture!'

'How?' I asked.

Michael looked at me in desperation. There was a flicker of anger in his eyes, but his body was too exhausted to mimic it. Then, visibly tired, he slowly said: 'I suppose I must work on my faith.'

Replacing what's good with what's right

Michael is a sensitive person. His deepest desire is to let God's light shine in his heart.

> If only I could … empty myself of everything that blocks God's light.
> If only I could … be free of the shame in my innermost being about who I am.
> If only I could … face the world with my head held high.
> If only I could … walk in God's truth, free from fear and judgement.

9

His battle is similar to the one that many others are fighting. He is an addict, trapped in the shame of his past that is causing shame in the present. Addiction represents a very strong kingdom, one that commands an army of obedient, fearful, misguided slaves. Unfortunately, addiction is often reinforced by words, especially if those words sound a lot like God's Word. Words bolster the belief that you will never be good enough and leave very little room for the truth about God's love and goodness. The broken spirit who teeters on the edge of giving up, is not helped by words like those that Geoff, Melody, and Stuart spoke. Instead, it is bound on both sides by two guards: Judgement and Shame.

Faith involves knowing the Person in whom you believe.

Only when Michael builds up enough trust to allow the truth of God's Word to enter his inner world, will he see freedom beckoning. When the Word is held up as a mirror to show him the original person God intended him to be, he will finally have a chance to escape his shackles.

However, it calls for an enormous realignment that will involve every aspect of his personhood. Once he finds the Living Word, the One who personifies wisdom, he will be able to start walking in victory. Only then will Michael be able to embrace re-creation and allow his inner wounds to heal.

Michael takes action

What helped Michael to take up his place in God's kingdom, was to stretch the concept of faith beyond himself. Faith is more than reciting Scripture verses or spending more time on devotions. It is more than 'standing on the promises' of God's Word. Faith involves knowing the Person in whom you believe, Almighty God, in such a way that you willingly invite his light into your life. (Part 2 will explain how to do this.)

Michael started to embark on journeys of trust. He started seeing himself the way his Creator does. He started to like himself. Eventually he allowed himself to heal.

When God's truth becomes your reality, re-creation takes place. Michael's willingness to open up and to listen attentively brought him to a place where God's truth could start transforming him, even though that truth contradicted all his preconceived notions and beliefs at the time.

He bravely revisited the traumatic events of his childhood. The more he talked through and worked through those events, the more he managed to surrender and let go, creating room for a new reality – one without judgement.

Victory lies in our discovery of who God is.

Michael's hope increased and his heart grew big enough to trust again, with God as his mainstay. Trust creates room for God's light to reveal all. His light exposes the lies. Every lie that held Michael captive was suddenly stripped bare by God's light. At last, Michael could see right through them. The confusion created by misguided religion could no longer bind him with feelings of guilt and shame. He discovered God's liberating grace and accepted his Heavenly Father's forgiveness and cleansing of his sins with a willing, no, an excited heart.

Ultimately, Michael forgave himself and confidently assumed his position as a victor in God's kingdom.

Conclusion

Religion without wisdom and goodness can have a profound effect, but it amounts to a false gospel. Undue emphasis is placed on the person and their inability to meet the high spiritual standard of the Bible. This leads to constant feelings of hopelessness, isolation, and guilt.

Victory lies in our discovery of who God is, and how He made a way for us to meet his kingdom's standards.

We must learn discernment if we want to avoid falling victim to spiritual manipulation or the abuse of human authority. As important as discernment is when we move in the world, it becomes even more important when we are at church or among church people. People with charisma and authority figures can play on our feelings of guilt and hinder our ability to discern between truth and falsehood. People's self-righteousness and religion without empathy can leave us confused and feeling judged, clouding our ability to experience God's love and goodness. If the Word is preached in an unwise manner, it can reopen old wounds, inflict new ones, and cause us to clam up.

It took great determination for Michael to reach out. Fortunately, he was desperate enough to keep on searching until fresh truth could permeate him from deep within. The change in him was sustainable.

MEDITATE A MOMENT

Take time out, settle your thoughts and think about the following questions.

- With whom do you feel safe? (Who are the people to whom you can tell anything without feeling judged?)
- Why do you feel safe with them?
- Whom do you trust most?
- Why?
- Do you know your own dark secrets? Write them down – for your eyes only.
- How hopeful are you that these secrets will be brought into the light to be solved? Answer on a scale of 0 to 10, where 0 is never, and 10 is most definitely.
- Will you share your secrets with members of your church/fellowship? Why or why not?

Prayer

*My King and Heavenly Father, thank you for inviting me to have
a relationship with You. Today I choose a relationship with
You over Christian service motivated by fear and guilt.
Help me to discern the harmful effects of false religion. I do not
want to be hurt by people who apply your Word without wisdom.
I confess that I can also be guilty of this.
Please equip me to shine your light on the lies that lead to
confusion and rejection, so that others may come closer to You.
Father, I want to come to you freely when I need clarity in my life.
I want to discard the mantle of shame that covered me, so that
I might walk in the healing, liberating light of your Word.
Let your truth become my own.
In the Name of your Son and my Saviour, Jesus Christ.
Amen.*

CHAPTER 2

LOOKING BACK

If only I ...
could change my past

A t the beginning of Genesis, we read: 'In the beginning God created the heavens and the earth' (1:1 NLT). God was there in the beginning, before there was a heaven or an earth. Before people. Before time.

We cannot imagine an existence without time. Time makes the progression of life measurable. We need a yardstick for beginnings and endings, moving forward and going back. This yardstick that measures past, present, and future consists of tiny time particles called moments.

We experience time as something that steadily moves forward, moment by moment. Each moment builds on the one before and influences the one that is coming next.

Certain moments leave deeper impressions than others – the day you wrote your final university paper, the evening you said 'yes' to the love of your life. Of course, also the moment you gladly surrendered your heart to Jesus, your Saviour, when you realised how much He loves you.

The burden of the past

Time is a mysterious concept – consecutive, dynamic, and completely out of our control. It is sobering to realise how unperturbed time marches on without an iota of help or control from us. People experience the passage of time in different ways. Sometimes time seems to stand still, at other times it simply flies by. We have different perceptions of time that often speaks more to our state of mind than to reality. Despite these perceptions and attitudes, time soldiers on.

Our universe is bookended by the dimension of time. Everything flows with it. For us, it is only logical. If you see two photos, one of an unbroken egg on the table and one of a broken egg lying on the floor, you would have no problem putting them in the correct sequence. First the egg was intact, then it broke.

> **There is a tug-of-war going on between the familiar places of our past and our uncertain future.**

The second law of thermodynamics (the study of the relationship between work and temperature) states that, in any system, entropy always increases, making the system less useful and more chaotic. This principle applies to the inevitable progression of time. Every moment, you grow older. Your body's available energy steadily decreases, needing more and more outside assistance to maintain more or less the same level as before.

Even though we cannot stop the march of time, nor do anything about time which has passed, the past never fully leaves us. The past influences the present. Experiences on our timeline inflict wounds that stay with us well into the future. That burden of pain from the past causes us to make choices in the present that are unwittingly driven by fear, or we make certain promises to ourselves because we are desperate to avoid recurring trauma. Both courses of action have enormous consequences, even though we only realise it when the chickens come home to roost. The result is a distorted perception of ourselves, God, and other people.

This bitter fruit keeps us shackled to the past, causing us to constantly turn back our gaze. Time and again, we look to the past in vain, because we are not prepared to face the current state of our lives. We remain trapped in regret, disappointment, and hurt of things that happened some time ago. It crushes our self-respect and messes with our perceptions. There is a tug-of-war going on inside us between the familiar places of our past and our uncertain future.

William's story illustrates how people can be trapped in the past even though they are desperately trying to escape it.

William

'Sir, I'm not sure when our next consignment will arrive.'

The annoyed shelf packer looked at the customer. What more is he supposed to say? He does not run the place. Eddie takes his dad by the arm and pulls him away, rolling his eyes. He knew his dad would cause trouble if he did not find the brand he was looking for in the shop. He needed to get his dad away from this place and somehow distract him.

William is a sturdy bloke and, as Eddie's friends would say, an angry old coot. William is not unaware of his rage issue. Sometimes it comes in handy, especially if he needs to get his way. Today he will control himself. He made a promise that he must keep, an agreement with his therapist. It was a bitter pill to swallow – the therapy, not the promise. He cannot believe that his wife, Marian, got him to agree to that. But he is a man of his word. He promised to go and give it a chance. For Marian's sake and for Eddie. Maybe for his own sake too.

When William first visited my consulting room, the room suddenly seemed too small, too full. It felt as if the furniture wanted to jump out the window. William had a larger-than-life presence. His eyes were full of pain and crying out for help. The man was desperate.

Coming to a therapist when you are desperate is a good thing, because desperation makes you willing to confront aspects of yourself. William's deepest hurt stemmed from his childhood when his dad imposed his warped ideas about manhood to him. When William angered his dad for any reason, his dad would put him in a grain-bag and hang it in the garage, where he would administer beatings and leave him to think about what he had done wrong. This happened often. William had to prove to his dad that he could take it like a man. That meant not crying, not becoming angry towards his dad, and not running to his mother to look for comfort. A man did not do those things, his dad would assure him.

William knew he could not be the man his dad wanted him to be. This left deep scars of rejection in his spirit. Consequently, he does not feel he can be the man Marian deserves, nor the dad that Eddie needs. The harder he tries, the more his 'dark side' comes to the fore. That is the reason why he agreed to therapy.

When he looks at me, his eyes say more than his words: 'You must help me with my temper. I fly off the handle and I hurt the people around me. A lot. I'm afraid I'm ... I'm ... going to lose them.'

'How do you plan to become the William you'd like to be?' I ask. He looks at me with a shocked expression.

'I thought you were supposed to be the one with a plan,' William says accusingly, but he manages to answer the question: 'I suspect my dad treated me wrongly. Now I ... I must deal with the consequences. If only my dad showed me how to be a dad with whom one could feel safe. If only he allowed my mom to comfort me ... Maybe it would've been better if one of my attempts at running away had worked.'

'How would that have made things better, William?' I ask.

'Maybe then I could have been the William I want to be.'

Time is always ahead of you

William feels sold down the river, and that makes him angry. He is angry about many things – his dad, his mom, the past. He is angry with God too.

But most of all, he is angry with himself. His disappointment at how his childhood experiences had robbed him of wholeness keeps the embers of rage smouldering.

> **Every day, you receive the brightest, most exquisite paint to colour your canvas anew.**

My heart breaks for the Williams of our suburbs, our churches, and our world. Many people are trapped in the prison of past experience, but nobody sees the steel bars that surround their hearts. What makes it even sadder, is that they helped to erect those bars. It makes them feel safe, at least for a while. Unfortunately, their emotions and behaviour will always look for a way out. The past is immutable. What happened, happened. The events are beyond our reach. Sure, they hurt us and left wounds that just will not go away.

Is there a way to fix the damage?

The things that happened are in the past. But your future lies ahead of you. And that is still pliable. It lies ahead of you like a big white canvas. Every day, you receive the brightest, most exquisite paint to colour it anew. You can paint or splash as much colour on it as you like. It is a choice, and the choice belongs to you. You are the one who decides whether you will simply mark time, live in the past, or embrace the future. If you do decide to move forward, you have options. Sometimes, walking into the future will make you feel vulnerable. It feels as if you are merely existing. Your progress lacks the freshness of the moment.

You need to realise that you can change your outlook. When you do, you will see wide open spaces around you; your troubled path will become an avenue of hope. You can follow this new path. You can change direction.

Let me illustrate it as follows: Your path through life is unique. It is constructed with a myriad of paving stones – big ones, small ones, wide ones, narrow ones. When you are hurt, your pavers lose their lustre and they become dull and grey. Your enjoyment of life is bleached right out of the stones. That does not mean that your stones are unacceptable and unusable. Do not fall for the illusion that you can simply walk away and collect new paving stones elsewhere and build a new road. Your dull, old pavers are precious and useful when you trust with childlike faith in God's ability to re-create. Something brilliant is about to happen. When you pick up your old pavers and turn them to the One who makes all things new, they change. God can cleanse you of sin and completely transform the paving stones on your path through life. He is at work, re-creating you. He transforms every lifeless paver into a shiny, precious stone. Your new path is strewn with emerald green, ruby red and solid gold pavers.

Is such a re-creation even possible? Suppose you cannot even see the dull, old stones from your past and you fail to evaluate the damage of your past experiences? How do you get there?

Open the door to the past

Imagine life as a long, dotted line. Every dot on that line represents one moment of William's life. The dots that represent the hurt from William's childhood flash red. They keep influencing his choices and behaviour. He cannot lay his finger on it, but he always feels as if an aspect of his being is malfunctioning. Before he can be whole and become the husband and father he longs to be, he needs to revisit those red lights. That is how the bars around his heart can be broken down. When William looks at those incidents and chooses to forgive, the Creator and King who is not bound by time, will release that hurt and with great empathy weave it into his dream for William's life.

The thought of forgiveness can be overwhelming. How do you forgive if you were a helpless victim? How do you forgive if the oppressor is still bullying you through snide remarks and rejection? The good news is that forgiveness does not depend on the other person's awareness of their sin, or lack thereof. Forgiveness does not depend on the other person and is not influenced by changes in circumstance.

> **God's truth needs to replace our skewed ideas of 'truth'.**

However, it is important to keep in mind that others' sin against you can have far-reaching effects. The poison of their sin can penetrate deeply and affect your entire person. Often, you try to protect yourself, but unknowingly, you are handing the keys of your free will to sin. This leads to immature and harmful behaviour. It makes you a carrier of other types of sinful poisons, such as bitterness or untapped potential. Eventually you do not even know why you are acting in such a destructive manner.

That is what happened to William. Fortunately, his desperation and loyalty to Marian motivated him enough to tackle the necessary changes.

William takes action

A key should fit its lock comfortably. If it does, unlocking is a mere formality. One important key on William's road to healing was the realisation that he had permission to live and take up space. The moment he realised the extent of his birthright, his heart was opened to a new identity. From that point he could start working on who William was when God created him. He could turn away from the abuse of his childhood and walk towards hope and resolution – away from pain, but without repressing, denying, or ignoring those painful encounters.

It did involve a period of confrontation. A person's hurts should be processed little by little. Only when William recognised how twisted and distorted his dad's ideas about male identity were, God's truth could start replacing those misguided notions. God's truth needs to replace our skewed ideas of 'truth'.

William carefully followed the steps to change which are described in Part 3, until his heart embraced this new truth. He learned to give himself the time and grace required to master this process. Eventually he knew the 'new' truth so well that he assimilated it into his life.

This brave man's road to healing was like a rough off-road trail, full of potholes and other obstacles. However, he persevered, and his loved ones were rooting for him all the way. It was a team effort, and the results benefited all the team members. I have great respect for the Williams in our society. Their determination gives new meaning to the term 'Braveheart'.

Conclusion

Your past lies behind you. Your past experiences lie within you. It can either poison you or strengthen you.

Can you change the past? No.

Can the damage of the past be changed? That is the right question.

MEDITATE A MOMENT

Pause with William for a moment and listen to your inner dialogue. If you could revisit your past …

- What would you change?
- Why?
- Where would you pause to gain better insight?
- Why?
- To what extent do you identify with William's story?

Prayer

*Lord, thank you for creating time in such a way
that I can only move forward.
I do not want to be held captive by the hurts in my past.
I do not want to waste precious time brooding over the past or
believing the lies those painful experiences are telling.
Will You, the Creator of time and the Re-creator of human beings,
please equip me to deal once for all with those painful memories,
and to get rid of the poison of sin that other people injected in me?
Please help me to cherish every part of my past and to see them as
opportunities to be re-created by You. Help me, Holy Spirit, as I
move forward through the process of forgiveness and repackaging,
until I taste the sweet victory that cost You your life.
In the Name of your Son and my Saviour, Jesus.
Amen.*

CHAPTER 3

LIFESTYLE

If only I ... improved my
diet, fitness, and meds

n Chapter 2 we said that we cannot change the past. When people realise that, they often decide to work on things they *can* change. They automatically focus on the things with which we are bombarded every day: physical appearance, lifestyle, health, fitness, even emotions.

Attraction and beauty are abstract concepts with no easy definition; usually it boils down to a mix of our culture and our value judgements. Research tells us that attractive people are generally seen as happier, more successful, and socially more acceptable than the plain Janes and Joes of the world. Being 'attractive' creates the impression that you are healthy and happy.

Society also equates attractiveness with success and social acceptance. However, what happens when you do not meet the accepted criteria for being 'attractive'? Then you – and your wallet – voluntarily become a slave to every marketer who convinces you that his product will help you make the cut.

Homo Sapiens (Pty) Ltd

In any business enterprise, it is crucial for the staff to understand and execute their roles so that the enterprise in its entirety can function effectively. Designated roles are very important to a company's functioning. The management team needs to take decisions and see that they are implemented. Workers must do their bit. There should be respect for everyone's rank and role. Every person has designated responsibilities, and if anyone fails to meet them, it means trouble – financial goals are missed, and a few years or even a few months down the line, the company may have to close its doors.

Individuals function like companies to a certain extent. Our psyche and body have a managing director, a board, assistants, and workers. If the team is managed well, it will run smoothly and effectively. We must pay attention to our health and physique too, but probably less than people think. As long as we know where they fit in, we can adjust our priorities accordingly.

Diet and exercise

Eating a slice of decadent chocolate cake with a good friend is better for my overall well-being than eating in a state of loneliness. That might sound controversial, I know. I feel that way, because I believe that safe friendships and a positive state of mind go a lot further in promoting inner peace and contentment than a healthy diet does. Of course, that does not mean that I am denying the important role of proper nutrition! But chocolate cake definitely has its place.

There is more than enough reliable research that touts the link between healthy eating habits and quality of life. Natural food that comes straight from the earth, clean water and the right exercise routine perform wonders for your body and your mind. Certain foods can even influence our mood.

There is also a fair body of research on the benefits of temporary fasting. When you fast for long periods, certain enzymes increase the hunger pangs you feel, because they activate the 'hunger neurons'. That can lead to obesity. However, fasting in a responsible, well-regulated way – e.g. for one day (eight to twelve hours) a week – will benefit you in a number of physical and spiritual ways. It works as follows: When you gradually condition your body to fast regularly, a chemical process is activated that is similar to your body's reaction to strenuous exercise. Research shows that a peculiar protein called brain-derived neurotrophic factor (BDNF) is released during aerobic exercise and intermittent fasting. BDNF supports the development of new thought patterns. Exercise and regular fasting also increase the body's production and secretion of serotonin (a 'feel-good hormone').

Regular, well-planned exercise helps your mind to replace old, musty beliefs with fresh, new ones. BDNF plays an important role in this process. When you exercise, this chemical substance increases in your brain's

26

hippocampus to support learning ability and memory-making. BDNF enhances your memory by strengthening the synapses (i.e. the tiny gaps between the terminal buttons of one neuron and the receptors of another neuron – see illustration below). It also promotes the growth of new neurons and supports the formation of connections between them.

This protein also stimulates the functioning of mitochondria in your cells. Mitochondria are sausage-shaped organelles that collectively form your body's chemical power plant. They play a key role in our general and mental health. When you have to exert yourself physically, these microscopically small machines can produce up to one tonne of energy.

Every cell's mitochondria contains enzymes that convert nutrients and oxygen into energy. Every mitochondrion contains a protein generator that is so small that 200 000 of them will fit onto the head of a pin. This little motor spins at 6 000 revolutions per minute to create the necessary energy. The motor consists of 31 different proteins. If you do not have them all, the motor will grind to a halt, and so will your body. The more mitochondria that are working in each cell, the more energy each cell releases to perform the necessary tasks. This automatically increase your feel-good sensations.

We need energy for our neurons to function. A neuron is a type of cell. It consists of a nucleus and several branches, and is responsible for the transfer of information in the body. The neuron's tree-like branches are called dendrites. They receive information from surrounding neurons. In turn, the axon that grows out of the neuron's nucleus transmit messages from the nucleus to other neurons. Your power plants are located along these axons. The older one gets, the slower the mitochondria are to move down the axon wall. The faster your mitochondria move along the axon, the quicker your neurons recover after an injury. The older one gets, the more difficult it becomes to recover from a brain injury.

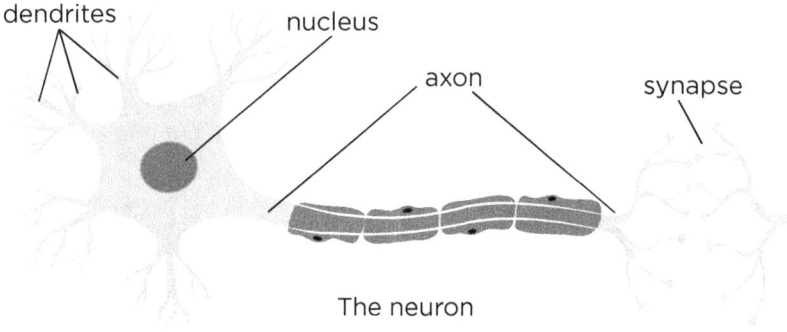

dendrites   nucleus   axon   synapse

The neuron

If you stop any jogger or cyclist and ask them whether they're grateful to be exercising, you will get a 'yes' every time. They are glad that they made the effort. When you finish exercising, the 'feel-good sauce' pumps through your veins for a few minutes and gives you fresh motivation to persevere. This chemical cocktail contains the wonderful neurotransmitter serotonin, as well as norepinephrine and dopamine. All three of them contribute to make you feel happy and content. A lack of exercise, on the other hand, causes strain on your body's systems and can steal some of your vigour, or even a lot of it.

> **We often need to pay attention to deeper aspects before true recovery will happen.**

A few minutes' exposure to sunlight every day also contributes to a positive mindset. The sun's ultraviolet rays stimulate the production of serotonin and its companion, melatonin. Our body releases melatonin when we sleep, especially if our surroundings are dark enough. When you go to bed, it is best to leave all the electronic devices that you work with during the day in your study. Rather resurrect your old, mechanical alarm clock.

The promised panacea of medication

It is alarming how easy it has become to use medication as the answer to any and all ailments. Society does its utmost to convince us that there is a tablet for every kind of problem – from a blocked nose to serious trauma. Medication can be a wonderful aid in recovery, but it can also be unnecessary and even damaging. Unfortunately, medication is seldom the complete solution or the blue skies at the other end of depression. At this point I must emphasise: There is nothing wrong with using medication, as long as we understand that we often need to pay attention to deeper aspects before true recovery will happen.

Let me explain it as follows: When your body 'talks' to you to indicate a deep-seated problem, it impairs your functioning. You cannot comfortably operate at the pace you normally would. Using medication when your problem is more psychological than physiological may help you to function normally and to start implementing the necessary principles for recovery.

But it does not address the whole, deeper problem. It is like a person who is driving somewhere when his vehicle's oil warning light comes on (see the illustration below). The light tends to distract the driver and can prove irritating after a while. So, to focus on the road, the driver covers the flashing light with a piece of masking tape. 'Much better!' he exclaims, rather chuffed with himself. Of course, somewhere down the road his car is going to come to an abrupt halt, because the problem (oil) has not been addressed.

Only so far

There are lots of things you can do to help lighten your mood: support-ive friendships, healthy food, mindful fasting, regular exercise, and moderate exposure to sunlight.

Unfortunately, the positive impact of diet and exercise cannot pene-trate your deepest hurt. It does not undo heartbreak and make you whole again. We are seldom prepared for the timing and circumstances of pain being thrust into our lives. When trauma strikes, our whole be-ing becomes involved. We automatically spend all our available energy on handling the situation. Our thoughts and feelings scurry around to restore a semblance of normality.

What happens when we experience trauma? There are various ways of handling it:

- You can quickly divide the events into facts and feelings and try to separate the two in order to restore or alleviate the damage.
- You can also bury the traumatic events so deep that it requires a lot of hard work to recall them.
- A third option is to immediately attempt to link the events to a ration-al explanation to convince yourself that a repeat is highly unlikely.

Unfortunately, emotional pain does not just go away.

The shortcomings of self-improvement

There are three things that will deny you the full benefit of regular exer-cise and a healthy diet: subconscious, unfulfilled desires; hidden sad-ness, and the fear of what-if scenarios. I have yet to meet a person whose dark soul stains were bleached even one shade lighter by diet and exer-cise. It may provide temporary relief, but not permanent change. For a while, your self-discipline and new programme might seem to hit the spot. You look good, feel good and have more physical energy. It cer-tainly helps a lot, but it does not wipe away the cobwebs in your mind. It also does not oust the eight-legged lie-monster. Between your denial and false beliefs, he is sitting pretty. And he will keep weaving his web.

Pain holds potential.

Initially, the brain does not distinguish between emotional and phys-ical pain. When pain strikes, the same parts in your brain are activated, regardless of the source. It makes no difference whether you hit your finger with a hammer or whether your best friend divulged your deepest secret. Pain is pain.

Research has uncovered a link between physical pain and relational pain. The study shows that certain processing functions which are associated with physical pain are linked to the amount of emotional pain a person feels during rejection. The degree to which that pain impacts you differs from person to person. When the brain receives pain messages, they usually get priority treatment over the body's other needs.

The word 'pain' is derived from the Latin word 'poena', which means 'punishment' or 'penalty'. It is interesting that suffering and the accompanying pain are often interpreted as punishment (especially on an emotional level). People wrestle with the whys and wherefores of suffering and desperately try not to be 'punished' again. However, the truth is that physical and emotional pain is often caused by others who sin against us, and that the victim's behaviour did not determine their conduct.

It is important to realise that pain also holds potential. Pain should not be seen as punishment or be interpreted in other negative ways. As long as you do not camp out in the pain, but process the whole experience effectively, it is bound to benefit you. The pain experience might even make you a better person if you process it well.

Pain has a ripple effect. The nature of that ripple effect is determined more by the way in which the pain is handled than by the pain itself.

Pain interrupts the normal rhythm of life. You must decide how much time and energy you want to (or should) spend on it. This is an important choice that is influenced by the content, intensity, and frequency of the particular pain message. Your age and your ability to process it also play a part.

When you go through a painful experience, the message goes from your senses to deeper within you in order to be processed. Your whole being is aware of and involved in the experience. Therefore, if you try to manage your pain (whether physical or emotional) on a purely physical level without factoring in (involving) the rest of your person, you are bound to end up in the ditch of disappointment.

Every time, you will place your hope on recovery in physical remedies, because you want to continue with life 'as normal', but you will run into a wall every time. The repeated disappointments can leave you downcast and too tired to try again.

Phoebe

It was a crisp day when Phoebe showed up at my consulting room, one of those days on which the sky seems bluer and the grass greener. It was as if the day's brightly coloured energy flowed into my office.

When Phoebe made the appointment, she said she had 'a few issues' to discuss. That was all. It was more like a debriefing, she said.

About ten minutes into the session, she was surprised by her own tears.

'I don't know what's the matter with me. Actually, everything is fine. I just need to sort out a few things. Where do these tears come from, all of a sudden?'

Almost annoyed, she wiped her tears and bundled up her tissues before throwing them into the dustbin.

'Look,' Phoebe said, ironing out a kink in her skirt, 'I think my life is almost where I want it. I just want to move it to a higher level of efficiency.'

'Why?' I asked.

'Shouldn't one always strive to improve? There is much more I feel I can and should do, but I just don't get round to it. Some mornings I even struggle to get out of bed. I think I'm just a bit tired. I don't sleep well.'

Her perfectly manicured hands reached for another tissue. She avoids eye contact while expanding on the disappointment she experiences over her current quality of life. Her mind is saturated with the poison of incessantly measuring what her life should be like, and the inevitable consequence thereof – disappointment. Phoebe's health and her state of mind are in a dangerous place.

'How would you like to move from disappointment to contentment as far as your quality of life is concerned?' I ask.

'I must keep on exercising hard. I simply have to push myself. And maybe I should get an antidepressant that won't mess up my metabolism. Or some good sleep meds,' she says, trying to sneak a peek at my reaction. 'Then I should be fine. Oh, and of course I need to keep my diet in check as well.'

Phoebe sits back, hopeful that she will soon be able to tick all the boxes.

A few months later we resumed her sessions. The poison of disappointment had seeped deeper into her soul and her feelings of self-worth had suffered even more. Phoebe's dream seemed more out of reach than ever.

False yardsticks

Weighed and found wanting. Time and again. Your inner scales are not going to change either. They cannot. The problem lies with your counterweights and the way the scale works. If only you can correct that …

The counterweights you so confidently place on one end of the scale consist of magazine images and movie plots. It is the friend who is always impeccably dressed and groomed, or the trophies and certificates your older sister or younger brother won. Or the accolades showered on other people at work events, just the way it worked in school. The same pattern. If only I …

At the other end of your inner scale is your accomplishments, the number of checkmarks on your to-do list, and your own convictions about all the things you have not achieved. The list of requirements Phoebe set for herself is very long. They weigh a lot. Daily, she adds new items to the list. Every day brings a new 'If only I can …' Still the scale will not balance. She never reaches her goal, despite the things she does or deny herself.

Phoebe needed to realise that the counterweights at one end of her scale were false measures of worth. However, the counterweights are not the problem. Neither are her efforts at the other end. The problem is that the scale is there at all.

Phoebe takes action

If Phoebe were a purely physical being, it might have worked to measure her worth with a scale. Maybe then she would not have struggled to reach her required standard of living. But Phoebe, like all of us, is far more complex than what we see on the surface. Her visible person is intertwined with her invisible components.

But that is not all. The role that each of these components play in making her life 'work' and filling her with joy is very specialised. If the Phoebes of the world want to hit their quality-of-life goals, they need to learn about and respect the role that each component of their person plays.

Phoebe managed to do that. When she started to understand the role and responsibility of the different components, she shook off the grip of the scale on which she weighed herself. That gave her the courage to devote her energy and focus to sorting out her inner world first.

She started to value all aspects of herself. Her conditional self-acceptance was replaced by unconditional, healthy self-love. Phoebe needed to do more than remove the counterweights. She needed to throw out the scale itself. Doing that is a liberating idea, yet daunting at the same time.

What did that do to the way Phoebe defined herself? Getting rid of the scale stripped Phoebe of the things that used to define her – at least in her mind. It also freed her of the conditions she placed on herself for acceptance. Over time her determination and abundant energy enabled her to reach her new goals – to truly get to know and love herself.

> **You were created to handle
> pain with respect.**

She learned to claim her right to just 'be'. The more she realised her value as a person, the easier it was to let go of the old counterweights one by one. She accepted a new self-definition that made the false identity yardsticks redundant. She also discovered that her identity is far more than other people's opinions or even her own conditional judgements. She had to discover her true self and let it sink in so that the truth of it could become hers. This process also taught her to be patient with herself – a very important aspect of self-respect.

I am proud of Phoebe and the road she travelled to get to the point where she could celebrate her uniqueness and really start liking herself. It made her appreciate the richness of life.

Conclusion

When you overestimate the role your body plays in your self-definition, you form a false image on the inside that leads to false expectations about life in general. You will pay more attention to physical (tangible) pain and neglect emotional pain – not only your own, but that of your children and friends. Your advice to people who experience emotional pain will tend to be 'Get over it', even though you will carefully attend to physical wounds. Fortunately, you were created to handle both kinds of pain with respect. To consider the whole person in all his or her wondrous complexity is an important condition of proper functioning.

Your body is the picture of yourself that you show to the world. We are bombarded by images of 'perfect' people, which places us under constant pressure to meet society's standards of acceptability. However, those images are distorted, like looking into a carnival mirror. The picture we see of ourselves does not tell the full story. Often, it causes us to feel despondent and dismayed, as if we somehow lack something.

However, you have the power to pause and reconsider. You can redefine your self-definition to include all your components. You can celebrate your marvellous complexity and live out your multi-faceted identity with renewed respect and understanding.

Re-creation thrives in such an environment.

MEDITATE A MOMENT

- What makes you feel better about yourself? Who makes you feel better about yourself? Why?
- When do you feel worthy? Why? Think of physical prompts, as well as circumstances, achievements, your career, and other aspects of society.
- What will become of you if you cannot meet these conditions that seem to give you worth? Who will you be if that happens? Why?
- To which degree do you identify with Phoebe?

Prayer

Creator God, thank you for weaving my body together so wonderfully. I do not want to neglect or disregard the visible part of my person. But I do not want to rate it so high that my physical needs become paramount to me. Forgive me for getting the balance between my body and my emotions wrong sometimes. I understand that it can waste precious energy and frustrate me. Please enable me to accept all aspects of myself, and to respect the way in which You put me together.

I would like to surrender my inner scale to you, and with it the counterweights I use to measure how acceptable I am. Please help me to patiently complete this process of surrendering and laying things down, until my whole being echoes your truth.

Thank you, King of the universe, for loving me unconditionally. Please help me to love myself unconditionally as your child, and to live out this love practically and with renewed understanding in terms of my focus, time, and energy.

In the Name of your Son and my Saviour, Jesus.

Amen.

CHAPTER 4

THOUGHTS

If only I ... could think
more positively

A s a child I regularly heard the story *The Little Engine That Could.* My mom was an excellent storyteller. She vividly coloured the images in my head with her warm voice, and her emphases and pauses did every sentence justice to give it maximum impact.

In a world of fast, fancy express trains, the little steam engine battled inferiority. As it happens, one day the fanciest express train ends up in trouble, and of course there is only one other train that can save the day. During its heroic rescue attempt, the little steam engine grows from 'I think I can, I think I can' to 'I know I can! I know I can!' At the end, he triumphantly crests the hill, the arrogant express train in tow.

The story's climax never failed to engender feelings of conquest and irrepressible optimism. I got the lesson: As long as I think I can, I can. My thoughts are powerful. The right thinking will boost me and help me to change. The moral of this story is indeed important, and I am grateful that it is a treasured part of my childhood memories. But much later my storyteller mom and I did go further down the little steam train's tracks.

The walnut-shaped organ

In the fourth century BC, Aristotle said: 'The brain is an organ of minor importance.' He reckoned its main activity was to cool the heat produced by the heart. Since then, our knowledge has expanded considerably. In the 1940s, Isaac Asimov declared: 'The human brain, then, is the most complicated organisation of matter that we know.'

Research on the brain has grown ever more specialised. Today we know that this organ – roughly the size of a cauliflower and weighing 1,5 kilograms – contains some 86 billion neurons (nerve cells). Neurons are Nature's smallest building blocks. They determine the nature of the things they build, so studying brain function needs to start with a study of these little particles.

Every neuron has branch-like connections to other neurons in its vicinity. These connections are responsible for the transfer of information and for memory. A description of all the connections of a single neuron will fill more or less 40 pages. If you want to document the potential branches and connections for all neurons, you will need a library with 10^{10} (ten billion) books!

Commands from the brain to the rest of the body are sent via these complex connections. The speed of the messages differs, but they can travel up to 40 metres per second (144 km/h). It is comparable to wind speeds in a hurricane.

People are born with a massive number of neurons, but few connections between them. The more branches and connections there are between neurons, the quicker incoming information is processed. Therefore, it is critically important to help babies form connections. Caregivers do this when they chat to and play with the baby, forge social bonds with it and teach it interesting things. Love-based behaviour towards a baby makes the bifurcations grow and stimulates the connections that are needed for effective development. When a mother or caregiver looks at a baby lovingly and makes strong eye contact, the brain produces very specific neurotransmitters. The brain is strengthened by normal, loving contact. It produces a chemical, oxytocin, during positive eye contact and loving physical touch.

Oxytocin is an important feel-good hormone that is released in the mother during breastfeeding and gentle touching. It helps with her recovery after birth. Oxytocin also serves to calm the mom and the baby. It helps to make the baby focused and teachable, which is necessary for healthy development. Additionally, all contact between mother and baby – touching, cuddling and verbal approval – serves to convince the child that he or she is worthy of love and respect. In turn, this promotes the ability to trust.

Every person wants to trust. Your ability to trust starts with your parents and their behaviour towards you. It creates your capacity for trust. The way your mom and dad look at you and talk to you (tone of voice and choice of words), and the amount of time they devote to you matter greatly. They carry important messages for your sense of worth and right of existence. It equips you to cultivate healthy relationships with your fellow human beings.

Positive feedback about small daily victories forms a very important foundation on which the child can build a healthy future. When a baby feels safe, secure, and loved, it enables them to tackle challenges that come their way and conquer them with flying colours.

Information is transferred electrochemically, and it is quite an impressive process. Chemical substances called neurotransmitters are among the main players in the communication process. They function almost like keys that unlock a protein gate in order for the information to continue its journey. The flow and processing of information deserve its own book, but what you should know for the purpose of our discussion, is that humans tend to be lazy. Or, to put a more positive spin on it, we like to conserve energy. Our cell-to-cell communication, therefore, does not use the way less travelled. Quite the contrary. Like the gazelle that follows the same well-trodden path to the waterhole every day, our brains first opt for the familiar, well-worn path.

When we receive incoming data, our brain prefers to process it according to its existing neuron map. That means that we react to a given situation in a pre-programmed way, according to our 'default setting'. This habit saves us lots of energy, but can also lead to very specific misinterpretations and leave us lost.

The limitations of positive thinking

In 1952, Norman Vincent Peale published his enormously popular book, *The Power of Positive Thinking*. Today the mantra 'If you think you can, you can' still reverberates around the world. Unfortunately, this type of thinking reinforces a specific perception about the importance of the brain in living a fulfilling, meaningful, high-functioning life. It places the main focus on our thoughts and the impact they have. In our efforts to improve our quality of life and get on the desired road to success, we end up almost worshipping our thoughts.

The result? We think we would be able to solve all our problems, if only we can think more positively.

It is said that positive thoughts will fast-track you on the road to success. This race leaves very little room for mediocrity or simply being good enough, let alone inferiority. Our weaknesses are denied any space.

That is how we are conditioned. Positive thoughts will enhance our lives and take them to 'the next level' in terms of our relationships, career, marriage, parenting, and even our immune system. All we need to do, is to identify, capture, deny, and remove the negative thoughts and replace them with positive ones.

There is nothing inherently wrong with this process. It can produce good results. In fact, it forms an important part of change. Then why do we struggle so, even though we read dozens of manuals and follow every five-step programme we come across? The only growth we encounter, is in the frustration and disappointment at our inability to become such positive humans.

> **An emphasis on positive thinking can, ironically, sabotage the very outcome it seeks.**

In our next case study, we meet Henry. He walked into my consulting room tired and despondent. Why? He was tired of struggling. Positive thoughts did not work anymore. The pursuit of success that was required by society, constantly touted by the media and repeated at social events only served to increase his feelings of failure. All the opinions and requirements burned in his heart. It left an indelible mark on his inner being.

Henry's story illustrates how an emphasis on positive thinking can, ironically, sabotage the very outcome it seeks. When your thoughts are the most important thing to you, it always complicates the implementation of your plan in the long term. It is like climbing a mountain with roller skates.

Henry

It is a hot day. So hot, it feels as if your flip-flops will melt into the sidewalk if you stand still for any length of time. On this swelteringly hot day, a man marches past the lethargic pedestrians and past shops, restaurants and offices. He's not wearing flip-flops. His black shoes, polished to a mirror finish, crunch on the sidewalk. Hot and annoyed, the tall man walks up to the hospital entrance. Henry's mother has been taken ill. Again. As usual, for him the timing could not be worse. He was working on one of his most important contracts so far, and that was not the only thing on his to-do list. He does not have time to deal with another crisis at the moment.

Doctor Milton extends a friendly greeting when Henry approaches and starts to explain things in his usual, measured way. Henry's not having it. He steamrollers the poor doctor with his signature blend of impatience and arrogance.

When Henry walks into his mother's hospital room, she looks at him apologetically.

'I'm so sorry, my child. I don't mean to trouble you. I know you're terribly busy ...'

She tries to make eye contact, but Henry is looking for a chair. He decides that he will stay for five minutes. That is what duty dictates.

'Yes, things are hectic,' he says as he sits down on the edge of the chair, cell phone in hand.

Why is it that this woman irks him so? Henry often wonders about this. He can't pinpoint the source of his inner conflict. He knows he ought to honour her as his mother, but every time she upsets his day, it drives him up the wall.

When Henry walked into my consulting room some time later, he was still fuming. His brooding 'let's just get this over with' attitude hung like a heavy trench coat around his summer body. 'This is never going to work,' I thought to myself. His coat of conditionality would have to go.

A well-tailored coat

All of us wear a coat sometimes. Not a visible coat, but the heavy, musty coat of our beliefs. We stubbornly cling to the 'truth' that we confess. We think others do not notice it when they pass by. But that coat, which we use to cover ourselves for years and years, becomes a hotbed of issues. Dark coats often cover frustration and a strong dose of discontentment.

We do not easily shed this coat, for two reasons: We may not even know that we're wearing it, or we just love to cling to it stubbornly. Such a coat becomes a hideout, a stuffy shelter that, strangely enough, makes us feel safe – safe in its predictability.

Henry will require great courage for the road ahead. He will have to ditch the coat and expose his inner vulnerability to the light so that he can look at the reasons for it. As the light penetrates his vulnerability, the healing will start. Light helps us to see what is really there. If there is not enough light, we shall keep on stumbling around in the dusk. Our preconceived notions will keep deceiving our eyes and our inner compass. In the One who made us, there is no shadow. If we ask Him, He shines the light of his Holy Spirit on our lives and opens our lives to his truth.

Realism vs. reality

Maggie and the girls had nagged Henry for a long time to do something about his negativity. She even got him to take a course on positive thinking. Imagine that!

Henry is a realistic fellow. He does not mince his words, and if he disagrees or is dissatisfied with something – which is most of the time – he will say as much. He believes that people should stop sugar-coating the truth, since it only creates false hope and fairy-tale expectations. No, he hates disappointment so much that he would rather prepare for the worst.

So I ask questions that will reveal his inner world a little more. Once he feels more comfortable, his words start flowing more freely.

> **We stubbornly choose to form associations that complement our perception of the world, rather than to be confronted by new possibilities.**

'I feel safe in my realistic world,' he says in summary. 'Define realistic,' I ask.

Henry is tired and hot, so I clarify my question: 'When, according to you, are you being "realistic"?'

Henry answers the question not just for himself, but for many of us. It is one of the core questions on your road to wholeness: Is experience the truth? Or is your experience your truth? When are you being realistic? Is it when you cling to the memory of your experiences in your soul's library? Or is it when you interpret things from your own personal experience? For example: A cold reception by your colleagues at your new job can confirm your suspicion that you do not fit in anywhere. Because you have been treated that way before. But is it always true? (Especially if your colleagues had just been informed of looming staff cuts.) Maybe you only start being realistic when you carefully analyse your sensory data and consider all the possible reasons for the set of circumstances. Using your heart's convictions, you can then carefully weigh each option while they are laid out next to each other, so that you can come to a responsible conclusion.

Our reality is shaped and reshaped by a wide range of factors, experience being among the most important. As we have said, our brain prefers the familiar, well-worn paths to arrive at what we believe and how we interpret a situation. We do not want to waste energy unnecessarily. That is why we sometimes choose not to process fresh sensory data from scratch, but rather to force it into the mould of our existing beliefs, our inner truth, so that we can confirm it: 'I knew it! Just as I expected!' In the meantime, our personhood suffers greatly. We deceive ourselves with all manner of lies and cling to them for dear life. We stubbornly choose to form associations that complement our perception of the world, rather than to be confronted by new possibilities.

Emotionally charged experiences usually demand our undivided attention and motivate us to use the required energy to process the incoming information. Such experiences play an important role when we have to make decisions in future. Your experience affects your choices. When an experience is accompanied by intense emotion, the impact goes much deeper. It becomes part of your beliefs. Thus, the experience's message, as interpreted by you, becomes your truth and your reality. In the third part of the book, we shall discuss why emotionally charged information receives more attention.

How does memory work?

Information from the outside world usually gets through to our inner worlds via the portals of our five senses. How we process that information defines our experiences and fills our memory bank. There is a number of ways in which we process our experiences and file them in our brain's memory bank. We are exposed to almost 10 million data bytes every second. All information is potentially important, so everything is filtered first to determine its importance. Almost 99% of incoming data is shelved by this process. It prevents a 'system overload' and gives the brain a break to file the rest.

In general, you get five types of memory:

- Episodic memory is the processing and reconstruction of experiences from our past. Our personal filters interpret those experiences and adapt them to the beliefs we hold.
- Semantic memory is what we use when we have to recite facts. It works without interference from our emotions.
- Working memory is the type of memory we use when we recall bits of information for a specific purpose.
- Procedural memory plays a pivotal role when we do everyday activities such as driving a car, walk or ride a bicycle. We recall the procedures we have learnt previously and execute them without much brain energy or focus. When you hold a book that you are reading, you are using procedural memory. The information in this part of your memory is constantly being replaced with the latest, most recent information.
- The fifth type of memory is implicit memory. This refers to data you can't readily typify or describe. We use our memory bank without really realising what we are doing and depend on our senses and associations to do it. These two have a subtle, often invisible influence on our opinions and behaviour. For example, they determine why you're sometimes nice to people, purely because they share a name with somebody you like. Of course, it works the other way round too.

Your truth

So, what is the truth? When are we being realistic? Einstein said reality occurs when one is able to predict the existence of an item or situation with certainty, without its composition (system) being distorted.

Each of us forms our own reality. That reality remains stable as long as your picture of normality is not drastically altered, i.e. as long as your familiar brain circuits remain passable, and you can reach your desired destination with little exertion. However, it is possible to be confronted by two contrasting choices at once. The resulting conflict forces you to choose between the two. What does that do to your perception of reality?

When we experience something, our senses interpret it on our behalf. However, this interpretation might differ radically from the true state of affairs. A good illustration of this dilemma is a young girl who is regularly physically abused by her dad. Instinctively, she knows that she needs a dad who can keep her safe and who can help her survive. This leaves her with two realities: The first is that she needs a safe dad, and the second is that her dad hurts her.

How can she make sense of her world while trying to process the abuse? She tells herself that she does have a safe dad, and that the cause of his callous handling of her could only lie with her. This belief shapes her reality, namely that his behaviour is her fault. She is the one who angers him, therefore the burden is on her to try harder every time not to provoke him. To the little girl, it is a survival technique that works, but it shapes her personal sense of reality in a specific, very distorted manner.

Why does Henry's sense of reality dictate that he should avoid disappointment at any cost? There is something about the experience of disappointment that he cannot endure. Henry's recovery will require him to conquer his fear of disappointment. To do that, he must find out where that fear comes from. Where did it originate? In Henry's case it was necessary to go back to his childhood and his relationship with his mother.

He found out that his mom had fallen pregnant with him when she was still a student. She was studying law, and her first two years had been a mix of diligent study and a vibrant social life. Then she met the man of her dreams. All of a sudden, she could think of nothing else but evenings with him and the wonderful future that beckoned for the two of them. She gave herself to him eagerly, but he did not keep his end of the forever-yours promise. Her parents would not support her either. Of necessity, she had to give up her studies and go look for work – not an easy task for a young, pregnant, single woman.

Those were the stressful circumstances of Henry's pre-born days in the womb. During his childhood he often received non-verbal – sometimes even verbal – messages of rejection. It was not that his mom did not love him, but her pregnancy and the difficult circumstances that accompanied it did not make for a warm reception. Subconsciously, she often wondered how her life would have turned out if she had not been saddled with a child.

Henry's friends and teachers constantly and vocally admired his sharp intellect and impressive talents, but nothing would convince him that he was good enough. Henry was angry with something or someone, and he himself topped the list.

Henry takes action

Henry's belief in realism and his efforts to practise positive thinking were like a house of cards. He stubbornly clung to his beliefs for a long time. It had become a kind of shelter for him. Eventually the wind of his frustration flattened his house of cards. His beliefs about reality had suddenly become invalid. He had to find a new definition of reality. He had to take a hard look at himself to figure out why his behaviour was hurting others. He had to go back to the place where he first donned that dark coat of his.

Henry had to hold his relationship with his primary caregiver, his mother, up to scrutiny. Her pregnancy turned her whole world upside down. She did not bargain on falling pregnant, and she was not prepared for the rejection by the baby's father and her parents. She had to give up her carefree student life and work hard to make ends meet for her and her baby. Even though she wanted to keep and raise her baby, the whole situation was still enormously disappointing. All her dreams were shattered. Her life did not turn out the way she had anticipated.

And into that situation, little Henry was born. No wonder he wore a coat of distorted reality from the very beginning. Henry and his mom did not form the bonds of trust that are supposed to develop between a mother and her baby during healthy cuddling. For the rest of his life, being with her subconsciously reminded him of this lack.

After a few sessions my client started to trust his inner world enough to discard the coat. It was a very brave step, but one that left his shoulders light and unencumbered. Henry could breathe, and he could reach Henry, the person. He was able to look at his wrong perceptions and warped interpretations of life, other people, and himself with new eyes. For the first time, he could truly forgive his mother, and his father too. He finally released himself from the reality that he created and believed about himself.

Conclusion

Your thoughts control your behaviour. Your behaviour determines your relationships. We all need positive relationships. We need it even more when we want to tackle and achieve change. Henry's wife, Maggie, played a huge role in Henry's recovery through wise, loving guidance and clear communication around what she found acceptable.

When you hurt important people around you, you and the people in question suffer great losses. But when they truly care, they are the ones who keep you honest. Hopefully, that will give you the motivation to change.

MEDITATE A MOMENT

Think about your reality.

- What is normal to you in your circles?
- What is your usual take on people? How do you see them?
- What do you think the future holds for you?
- What would you rather avoid: failure, disappointment, punishment or rejection? Why?
- In what order would you list these? (Which one do you avoid the most?) Why?
- What happens when people close to you criticise your behaviour? How does that impact you?
- Which aspect of Henry's story hits closest to home for you?

Prayer

*Thank you, Lord of my life, that I consist of more than a brain
and some thoughts. I know my being is much more complex.
I know I cannot focus only on thoughts and emotions if
I want to live a victorious life.
Father, teach me who I really am and what I am made of. Please
equip me to live out your principles from a place of deep
conviction. Show me the things in my life and my past that I need
to let go and that must be renewed. Help me so that my capacity
for your truth can increase. I know that You, Holy Spirit, are
burning to help me with these things.
I choose your truth over my own interpretation of reality.
Re-create my total being, Lord, so that I will constantly
be aligned with your truth.
In the Name of Jesus, my Saviour and Re-creator.
Amen.*

CHAPTER 5

ACCEPTANCE

If only I ... could be **acceptable**

My mother was a master at showing unconditional love. Her joy when I entered her room fuelled my heart's engine, even when she was suffering from cancer. It is that exact expression – pure joy – that a child is looking for in his mother's eyes when he gets into the car when she picks him up at school. Are you glad to see me? Do you enjoy being with me? A parent's face is carefully scrutinised, and the non-verbal messages land deep in a child's heart. When love and acceptance are not given unconditionally, one's self-definition becomes conditional, prompting you to look for measurable qualifications all the time. What must I do to be worthy and acceptable – or just good enough?

Remarkable people's stories do inspire, but when you compare yours to theirs, it can be very demoralising. You wonder how you compare. How far am I off the mark? How long before I get to that level? In our society and environment, we are confronted with all kinds of demands and requirements. We measure ourselves by all the colourful photos of the ideal lifestyle and achievements.

The pivotal question is: Who are you when you cannot achieve all those things? What determines your value?

Cups of need

When you start digging in a broken person's life, the foundation you often get to is rejection. People want to be accepted. When we are weighed and found wanting, we can't be whole.

We instinctively know that it is hugely important to experience un-conditional acceptance in the womb and the cradle already. It is as if we arrive in this world with a number of tiny cups. These cups are empty and are supposed to be filled by our primary caregivers. They should fill our need cups out of their own overflow.

A young child's cups that typically need filling are:
- to feel that they matter;
- to feel physically, emotionally and spiritually safe, and to feel provid-ed for;
- to receive recognition for everyday achievements;
- to be treated with compassion and respect;
- to know that their lives have a glorious goal, and
- to feel good enough, even when they make mistakes and reveal their shortcomings.

This list of needs can be summed up in two words: unconditional love. We need to hear that we are 'enough' just because we are here. Unfortu-nately, our primary caregivers do not always have full cups themselves. They try so desperately to get their own cups filled that they have no energy left to fill those of others.

The first three years of a child's life are crucial.

When children are deprived of the safety of unconditional love for any reason, it makes them anxious about life's demands and about their future. Subconsciously (and sometimes consciously) they are driven to less wholesome life choices. Since their basic needs are not being met, they look for ways to fill their need cups. They want to fit in. They want to feel safe in their environment. Unfortunately, most efforts to fill their cups lead to recurring disappointment and, sometimes, despair.

The first three years of a child's life are crucial, because that is when certain very specific brain circuits are formed. These circuits should lead the child away from negative emotions such as anger, frustration, sad-ness, jealousy, fear, pain, and shock, and bring him or her to the positive emotion of joy instead. In other words, a child should learn to process negative emotions in a positive way. When parents or caregivers com-fort children after they take a tumble or distract them when another child has said something hurtful, the good circuits are reinforced. I am talking about the circuits that lead to your place of rest and recovery. It is the place of joy. If you build this circuit and reinforce it often, joy will become your dominant emotion. As you mature into adulthood, recovering after disappointments gradually becomes easier. Finding your joy again does not take quite so long. This good place of rest becomes the default station where you stop and recover after an upsetting experience. It boosts your confidence in your ability to seek and find your own solutions for recuperation. It establishes healthy resilience and confirms our belief that our actions play a large role in the outcomes of our lives.

If you were not privileged enough to develop such a resting place, such a wellspring of joy, your brain likely mapped out some other routes that are supposed to lead to recovery. However, alternative recovery routes are often harmful, because they are rooted in bitterness, rebellion, or self-pity. Other unhealthy avenues include performance-driven behaviour, aggression, and arrogance. Your own efforts to get your cups filled often lead to these. Neither rest nor peace resides there, but restlessness and discontentment do. There is a deep yearning within you that you can't quite define, and it leaves you vulnerable, unfulfilled, and frustrated. You are always chasing something else, something more. And before you know it, the negative behaviour that led you to this place starts all over again.

Michael, about whom we read in Chapter 1, and Michelle, whose story we're about to learn, illustrate this dilemma well.

My cup overflows

Sometimes it is good to consider that we carry the life of our Creator God inside us. He, the Source of all life, breathed into your lungs. He gave you life, and He said that his creation was good. That in itself should shore up our feelings of worth.

> **God's unconditional love can fill even the tiniest need cup in our cupboard to overflowing.**

David did not have an easy life, but he knew to Whom he could turn when problems threatened. He was in the valley of the shadow of death, yet he could sing: 'You prepare a table before me in the presence of my enemies; You anoint my head with oil; My cup runs over' (Ps 23:5). David understood how dependent he was on God, and that God would never leave him nor forsake him. He knew that he could count on God in every circumstance.

Trusting God enables us to obey Him and to submit to Him. This is how we align ourselves with God's intentions for us, and with his provision. In turn, that stretches our ability to receive his truth.

He fulfils all our needs. His unconditional love can fill even the tiniest need cup in our cupboard to overflowing. He is enough. More than enough. He is El Shaddai, God Almighty. This deep assurance strengthens us when we realise that He will continue to fill our cups. It does not have to stop. Ever.

Michelle

The restaurant is packed. Michelle is grateful for their table in a quiet corner. She finds it increasingly hard to handle the noise in busy public places. She taps on the table with her nails, her gaze fixed on the entrance. When Peter walks in, she smiles relieved. He spots her immediately and walks over with fast, confident steps.

He greets her and says: 'Wow, you look gorgeous!'

Michelle's eyes flicker and she bites her bottom lip. Why can't she just say, 'thank you'? He is so good to her. She and Peter met three years before and have been married for a year now.

Peter looks at her with concern and sighs before he can help himself. 'Hey, Mich. Will you please make that appointment? You can't go on like this.'

She assures him that she has made the appointment already. She hopes that she will find a solution to her problem this time around.

Michelle is one of those beautiful women that you cannot help but admire. She is spontaneous, friendly, and naturally people-oriented. Her self-assertiveness is admirable, and she is successful at work. If you are looking for a template for the ideal woman, her appearance would come pretty close. So why is her life falling apart?

'My headaches are stealing my life. I have tried everything. Nothing is helping.' Michelle sits in my consulting room. Her appearance is impeccable, but her face is buried in her hands. She looks up. Her eyes are pleading for some sign of hope. She tells me about her life, but I cannot find any loose threads that could possibly lead to the cause of her headaches. Her tales are of a happy childhood, the first netball team, leadership positions, many friends, a happy marriage, and extended family who keep in touch. The array of medical tests also offered no substantial diagnosis.

After a few sessions, we start to go deeper. We talk about the upcoming Christmas holidays – a time for family, but also a time to show that you measure up. Like a dam wall that bursts, the carefully constructed wall around Michelle's heart collapses. She talks about the regular stomach cramps, night sweats and emotional turmoil that crop up before Christmas each year.

'Imagine you're sitting in your parents' home with your first cup of tea. What is happening?' I ask.

In her mind, she goes to the familiar lounge with the ticking grandfather clock and the heavy curtains.

'My mom is talking about Esther's achievements. "Esther just finished this project. Esther works so hard. Esther this, Esther that!"'

It is as if the opportunity to air her repressed thoughts brings renewed anxiousness. Her place as second best of the two sisters is firmly cemented in her mind. That is her truth.

'It doesn't matter what I do. I never seem to measure up to Esther!'

Michelle tousles her stylishly cut hair. Every now and again, she frowns and hesitates. I gently encourage her.

'Do you feel "less than" when you visit your parents?'

'Ever since I can remember,' Michelle continues, 'my mom wanted me to be more like Esther. And I fell short in every respect. I didn't make the Boland netball team. Esther did. I could not bag a man with as many degrees as Esther did either. On the few occasions when I did come home with a trophy or a certificate, Esther would be there already with an even bigger accolade! Eventually, I didn't even bother anymore. I gave up on the idea of ever making my mom proud of me.'

'What would your mom's approval mean to you, Michelle?' I ask.

She blows her nose with less inhibition than the previous time and holds on to the tissue.

'It would make me more like Esther. I would feel happy. Maybe I would even like myself! Instead, I feel like someone who is bobbing around on a cold, infinite ocean. I feel lost, and the worst is that I ... I ... hate my mom.' Her last statement barely rises above a whisper.

Silence. Suddenly Michelle leans forward, her hand reaching for her handbag.

'I can't say things like that! I'm supposed to honour my parents! This just proves how horrible I am! What if ...'

'Finish that sentence, Michelle.'

'I can't.' Inside Michelle a battle rages between denial and confrontation. This time, confrontation wins out. Michelle looks at me hesitantly and scared. Then she says barely audibly: 'What if I am the person my mother thinks I am?'

'And how would you answer that question?'

I see the fear, confusion, and desperation in her eyes.

'Then I will never be acceptable. Then I'm just a massive disappointment as a person.'

Your body's language

The moment you verbalise the things you fear the most, it is as if you're breaking a chain around your heart. You can see what happens after you push the words out and put them on display.

Michelle's battle is a good example of how your body can force you to do some soul searching. Her body started to cry out and forced her to take a look at the invisible reality of her inner world. We are quick to run to the doctor when our body gets sick, but we drag our feet when it is time to pay attention to the problems of our inner being. We ignore the red flags in our hearts, and over time our defence mechanisms become embedded habits. We learn to deceive ourselves with 'everything's fine'. However, all the red flags that we ignore eventually become blaring claxons that find tangible expression in our bodies. Michelle started to get inexplicable headaches. Her body kept talking until her lifestyle of pretending, resisting, and persevering was not working anymore.

Fortunately, her husband cared enough to plead with her to go for help. And she was willing to go the route of self-scrutiny. She learned to discern and respect her body's language. In fact, she learned to love and respect all of herself. She increasingly started to recognise the bonds of fear in her relationships. Over time she replaced them with bonds of love, and her need for acceptance with self-acceptance. All her relationships were impacted: with colleagues, friends, her husband, and herself.

Michelle's honest assessment of her mother's role in her life and the injustice that she suffered was liberating. When she reached that point, she could receive God's truth, even though she was sometimes tempted to turn back to the need for parental acceptance.

Mirrors of life

What lay ahead for Michelle now that she had answered her 'What if?' question and laid bare her fears?

Her first order of business was to determine why the annual family gathering upset her so. Christmas is a time of expectation. Families and relatives make plans to get together. Everybody bakes and cooks and shops. People like Michelle hope that the gathering will fall through or, if it does not, that it will pass quickly. For Michelle, the expectation brought confrontation. When the family got together, she could see what everybody's expectation was – and how she did not measure up.

> **Not every mirror you look into gives
> a true picture of reality.**

When we encounter people, it is as if each one holds up a mirror in front of us. In it, we see ourselves through their eyes. We see the expectations they have of us and the value they attach to us. The image we see (or think we see) in the mirror forms part of how we picture ourselves.

The way caregivers react to a baby's cries for help or attention, plays an important part in the formation of the baby's self-image. When caregivers eagerly and lovingly rush to help the baby, when their love is evident in the way they handle it, the baby sees an image in the mirror that says he or she is very valuable. Such babies learn that they are people who are worthy of a respectful response when they express a need. They have value. Therefore, they approach the future gratefully and confidently.

If the caregiver who reacts to the baby's cries is impatient, irritated, or even rough, the baby learns that it has little value. They approach life anxiously, without love and respect to buoy them. The same happens when the baby's cries for help are ignored. The image the baby sees in the mirror is not a pretty picture. It confirms their fears.

When we grow up, the original image that we saw in the mirror stays with us, etched into our minds and sealed in our hearts. This deep conviction of who we are and who others are, controls our thoughts, our will, choices, emotions, and behaviour. We are the result of the images in the mirrors that have been held up in front of us.

As a child the fun fair was an exciting place that sold candyfloss and popcorn. The greatest fun was to be had in the tent with the chamber of mirrors. The mirrors all reflected skewed images that pulled your face and your body completely out of proportion. Some mirrors made you look impossibly tall and thin, while others shrunk your head and gave you a bowling ball body. One breathed an involuntary sigh of relief when you stepped out of the tent, grateful that you looked nothing like the images in the mirrors.

The mirrors that people show us – and that we show to people – are like the mirrors at the fun fair. Their surfaces are bent and the images they reflect do not represent the truth.

Not every mirror you look into gives a true picture of reality. Often you see a distorted picture of yourself and your value. However, when your first glance at such a distorted image happens in early childhood, you believe in that image wholeheartedly. You grow up with that memory, not even considering that it could be wrong. Sure enough, your experiences confirm the 'truth' of what you saw and still believe. Your established circuits are constantly reinforced by every occurrence of inconsiderate, impatient, irritated, and insensitive behaviour you encounter.

That is what happened to Michelle. Every time her mother compared her to her sister, the 'truth' that she was not good enough was reinforced. Every time she encountered a negative reaction, her false perception of being 'less than' grew stronger. Because she believed in it so strongly – that brain circuit had become a six-lane highway – she could not believe any positive reaction that came her way. They just had to be wrong. But, in her mind, her first caregiver could not be.

Two types of trauma

There are two types of trauma. Type A trauma takes place when you do not get the type of treatment you are supposed to. Neglect and emotionally distant care count themselves under this type. Type B trauma happens when you are actively harmed, for example when you are physically, sexually, verbally, or emotionally abused.

In our relationships with other people, we often fall into a specific pattern that typifies most of our relationships. The type of connection we form with our parents or first caregivers, becomes our spontaneous, involuntary reaction. It becomes our standard relationship that forms the template for all our other relationships, often without us being aware of it. Relationships that are built on love promote honesty, transparency, and intimacy. Such a relationship consists of loving bonds between the relevant parties. Naturally, one likes to spend time with someone with whom you feel a love connection. Also, you do not mind if that person can see everything that's going on inside you, including your weaknesses. You do not fear rejection, because it is not on the menu. Such a relationship always makes you feel safe and secure.

> **When you fully and unwaveringly trust in your Creator, you can enter into his rest.**

When your behaviour in relationships focuses on avoidance, chances are that you are being motivated by fear. Because you fear that the relationship will not work out, everything you do is driven by the desire to avoid disappointment. You can't imagine revealing your real self to the other person, because the potential negative consequences are just too scary. A person can fear different things – abandonment, rejection, or punishment. When a humiliating experience has impacted you very deeply, you will avoid all situations that can lead to the same embarrassment. You might think that you are safeguarding yourself, but in reality, you are boxing yourself in and sacrificing quality of life.

Michelle takes action

Michelle's relationship with her mom was based on the fear of rejection. It had become her standard type of relationship and formed her template for future ones. What would happen if someone came too close and saw the real Michelle? She feared rejection from others, because it would confirm her mother's opinion. And she couldn't bear that.

Michelle is a lovely person. Her husband, her friends, and her colleagues often tell her how great she looks and how good she is at her job. But the words never make it to her core. She does not have the type of inner glue that makes good news stick. Her bonds of fear keep her isolated, and she goes to great lengths to keep people at a safe distance. Michelle struggles to feel adequate and loved in any relationship. Peter battles daily to assure her that he loves her unconditionally. She does not have the inner capacity to experience that kind of love.

Fortunately, that can change. When you fully and unwaveringly trust in your Creator, you can enter into his rest. When you're safe in that resting place, his light can penetrate your deepest recesses. His Word of truth can do its masterful surgery. That is change that lasts for eternity.

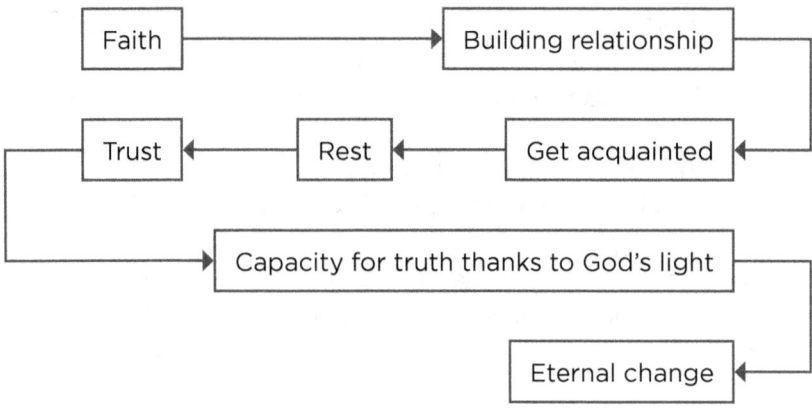

Michelle had to work through the sobering reality that her mother was unlikely to ever accept her the way she was. This process requires a form of grieving, but it is necessary if you want to be at peace in the situation, and if you want to transfer your expectations to matters that do fall under your control. Michelle tackled this grieving courageously.

She had to accept that there is only one mirror that shows her what she is truly like – the mirror of God's truth. In the mirror of God's loving gaze, Michelle can see her infinite value to Him.

In other words, there is only one reflection that shows us what we really look like. That image calmed the storm raging inside her and eventually became her reality too. The more she discovered her worth and identity, the better she could see it in the mirror of her husband's behaviour towards her, and the more she could accept and enjoy his love.

Conclusion

Emotional ties are formed between a baby and its caregiver during every interaction. The way the caregiver handles the baby conveys whether the caregiver assigns worth to the baby or not. When the verbal and – vitally important – non-verbal communication is negative, the baby's needs are not met. That results in trauma. This trauma surfaces in later life when the person struggles to build meaningful relationships. Ultimately, healing is only possible if the person reacts to their body and spirit's cries for help and seeks counsel. Each one of us needs to discover the truth – that we are important to God. We are precious in his sight. We do not need people to hold up mirrors for us. In God's mirror we are beautiful.

MEDITATE A MOMENT

- What do you hear when you listen to your body's language?
- What do you think when you look at yourself in the mirror?
- What thoughts regularly go through your mind? Whose voice do you often hear in your head?
- How do you describe yourself and your place in the family you grew up in?
- Is joy your default resting place?
- How do you recover after an unpleasant experience? Where do you go to recuperate?
- What are your needs? Which of your need cups need filling?

Prayer

*Creator God, You knit me together. I can't hide anything from You.
Still, You say in your Word that nothing will separate
me from your love.
You want to have a relationship with me, regardless
of my outer or inner condition.
Thank you that I am always welcome to share my heart with You,
without fear of rejection. Please help me, Heavenly Father, to be
honest. Help me to be open with You and with myself, especially
about the things I keep twisting. I want to get rid of my false hopes.
They offer no peace, only recurring disappointment. Today I
choose to lay them down, even if it makes me vulnerable, so that I
can make room for your truth and develop renewed trust in You,
the only One who will never disappoint me.*

*Creator God, forge in me a new path to a place of rest and joy
where I can go after experiences that leave me reeling.
Introduce me to your joy, Lord.
Help me to trust You to make my joy complete and
to grant me your peace.
In the Name of your Son, my Saviour, Jesus.
Amen.*

CHAPTER 6

OTHER PEOPLE

If only I ... could
change my circumstances

The dance of life is always a group act. Sometimes our contact with the other group members is full of purpose and energy, at other times it is casual and fleeting. It can have a big impact on our lives, or it can scarcely affect us. Whatever the case, energy is exchanged.

In 2006, Microsoft analysed 30 billion electronic conversations among 180 million people as part of a 'small world' study. They concluded that, on average, any two of those people could be linked by a string of fewer than seven acquaintances. If you have a smartphone, there are fewer than seven people between you and any other smartphone owner on the planet.

This much is clear, with or without a study: We are social beings. Our humanity is inexorably tied to the humanity of other people. You influence the people you come across, and they influence you in turn. When children grow up in a stable environment, their contact with other people is safe, orderly, and under control. Their parental home is a haven, and the routines are regular and predictable. Life holds no threat for such children.

Unfortunately, at some stage we all need to leave that safe cocoon, after which our safety cannot be guaranteed any longer. All of a sudden, we have to learn to secure our own environment, or at least the part we can control.

You and your environment. Who influences whom? Are we the product of circumstance and/or genes, or are people more complicated than that? If you think of yourself as merely the sum total of your circumstances or genes, you can't help but feel exposed and vulnerable.

If your relationship ties are based on fear, it becomes extremely important to you to avoid negative outcomes. People like this dread situations like rejection, disappointment, punishment, and conflict. Those fears become the driving force of their behaviour. They do the dance of denial or avoidance and are constantly walking on eggshells. Their uncertainty keeps the fear alive, which prevents them from focusing on workable solutions. They do not feel in control. They feel abandoned and hopeless.

Before they know it, they're living in survival mode, struggling to keep on keeping on. They bury their dreams, interests, and talents in a deep hole, so that they won't be reminded of the loss every day. But their hearts and emotions keep haemorrhaging.

Never silence the voice in your heart.

It is the haemorrhaging that keeps their anger going. Fear and anger are like a hammer and nail – frequently found together. When somebody gets hurt physically or emotionally, they get angry. Their anger serves as a kind of protection. They somehow believe that they will avoid similar situations more readily if they remain angry. Such a belief does not deliver the desired outcome, however, because anger (combined with unforgiveness) cannot really protect you, regardless of how tenaciously you cling to it.

Then there's the added problem of discerning your own voice in the throng of voices rushing at you from your environment. Voices of society, voices from the culture, voices from your family, friends, and acquaintances – these voices are so loud and urgent that they often drown out your own voice, albeit subtly. Without you noticing, the external norms that are forced upon you become your own norms. You want to fit in, be part of, and feel included and accepted. Consequently, you start giving in to outside demands. Before you know it, your efforts to fit in become your greatest trap.

You start relying on denial to get you through the day without a meltdown. You deny the abnormal state of your existence. It becomes a habit, something you put in place without too much thought or energy. However, it is the start of a vicious, destructive cycle. When you constantly make excuses for loved ones who wrong you or others, just so that no one will rock the boat, you become an accomplice. You keep mending and hiding while praying that no one will look behind the curtain you are holding up. There seems to be nothing that can stop the guilty person. He or she continues on their trail of destruction, apparently unhindered.

Nobody ever does this purposely. On the contrary, they think they're doing it for the sake of peace and progress: I just want to create a stable environment for the children. After all, isn't it noble to absorb all the unpleasantness and form a buffer to protect the innocent (often the children) in my life? Unfortunately, such behaviour achieves nothing; it only creates room for more problems. In the blink of an eye, you've sacrificed your identity. You forget that, through your silence, you are evading your responsibility towards your family.

Solutions and true peace will only emerge once you start listening to your inner voice and begin to discern between your responsibility and other people's, your sin and other people's. Here's the point: Never silence the voice in your heart.

Rita was brave enough to pull away the curtain in front of their family's picture-perfect pretend life. I am proud of her and other people like her, who tackle denial and avoidance head-on and ditch them for good.

Rita

'Quick! Jump in. Get your feet off the seat! Have a quick bite. We're almost there.' Rita shoves a cheese sandwich in her 11-year-old son's hand.

They're rushing. Again. This time from his school to the sports field for some terribly important match. Then it is on to the other school to pick up their daughter for her piano lesson, before returning to fetch her son after the game.

And so it goes every day, from dawn until dusk. Weekends are not much better. Rita's husband, Klaus, is a social person who loves organising get-togethers. Klaus is also a man with very little patience. His fuse is short, and his humour is mostly at the expense of others.

Rita and Klaus have been married for fifteen years, but Rita sometimes wonders about Klaus's definition of the word 'married'.

His approach to spousal communication is: 'Do it my way, or else.' And the 'else' is never pleasant. They have two talented, active children: the 11-year-old Friedel and the 13-year-old Liezel. Fifteen years of marriage had taken its toll. It felt much longer. Years of struggling to keep all the balls in the air while shielding her children from trauma showed itself in her posture.

Rita is tired. Actually, she's exhausted. She is way past worried or despondent. Even past crying. To her, between driving mom's taxi, keeping up appearances in front of the other moms, and cooking and entertaining over weekends, surviving is a full-time job.

Rita only woke from her slumber of denial when Liezel had her first close brush with her dad's temper. When she walked into my consulting room, she told a story that is all too familiar to many women.

'Tell me about the most recent incident,' I say during one of our sessions. Rita chooses that fateful evening.

'I can't believe you're complaining about being tired again, Rita! It's all you do! Complain, complain, complain! You know what? I'm starting to feel embarrassed about inviting people here! When last did you take a good look in the mirror? You look like a hag!'

Klaus's loud tirade was not confined to their bedroom walls anymore. It felt to Rita as if it reverberated through the whole house. Klaus was on a roll, helped in no small measure by a few rounds with his drinking buddies. Rita tried to calm him, but that just seemed to aggravate him more. Liezel probably heard them, because her music got louder all of a sudden. Klaus isn't exactly fond of loud teen music. He opened the door and started shouting at Liezel. That was the moment that shook Rita out of her covered-up existence.

Liezel came out of her room. Her face was a mixture of fear and anger, but she was ready to take on her dad.

'Klaus, please!' Rita pleaded. He did not even hear her. In a desperate attempt to get her husband away from their daughter, Rita grabbed Klaus by the arm. He swung around furiously, striking Liezel hard. She hit the wall, and the next moment his forearm was at her throat. Rita watched helplessly as Liezel wriggled herself from his grip and ran down the hall hysterically. All they heard was the front door slamming shut.

'How do you want to continue, Rita?' I ask.

Her tired eyes looked at me like a prisoner's would.

'If only …' She hesitates, staring in front of her. Then she says, ever so softly: 'If only … Klaus would change.'

Invisible boundaries

You live on an invisible piece of land. The land belongs to you. To you only. Your garden, your home, your furniture. There is a fence around this piece of land, and it has a gate. The gate is important, because it has to remain shut until you yourself decide for whom you want to open it. Sometimes you might chat across the fence with a curious passer-by or a potential friend. Sometimes you say goodbye to a person and watch them go; sometimes you decide to open the gate and let the person in. The choice remains yours, not the other person's. You also get to decide how far the person may enter. You are in control of the fence and the gate and the piece of land.

I do not often see five-year-olds in my practice. I usually refer them to a play therapist. One time, however, I changed my rule and saw a very special little girl. We immediately had a good rapport, so I decided to give it a few sessions. I asked her to draw me a tree. I gave her a blank sheet of paper and some bright pastels. She drew a tree with wide, open branches, a bird sitting in a nest, and grass growing around the trunk. Her tree was firmly rooted in the ground. She felt confident that it could survive a big storm.

'So, is this tree perfectly safe?' I asked.

She shook her head. 'What if a woodcutter tries to chop my tree down?'

She could not have that. The tree (which represented her) had to keep growing and remain safe while her parents were getting a divorce. The two of us had to come up with a plan to make sure that her beautiful tree stayed intact. So, we saw to it that her tree got a sturdy fence around it, with a gate on one side. Nobody but Jesus was allowed to enter through that gate! And nobody was allowed to come near the tree without Jesus's permission. Finally, her tree was safe.

All of us need such guarded fences. And we need this Guardian, the One who does not sleep or slumber.

Rita had to acknowledge, understand, and take back her territory. All invaders and squatters had to go. She had to gain a new understanding of where her boundaries lay and who she, Rita, really was. Only then could she begin to fix her fence. And after that, she could start tending the land.

Your territory belongs to you. It encompasses all that is within your control and everything you are responsible for. When you accept responsibility for something beyond your control, you are wasting your energy on unnecessary things. So, what falls within your territory? Your time and your choices. Your choice of friends, interests, and your faith. Your attitude, thoughts, and emotions. How you behave and how you handle situations. These are the things you have to take responsibility for. They are yours to control.

> ## The ability to choose is one of our strongest powers.

You cannot blame other people for your choices, emotions, behaviour, or attitude. You alone are responsible for them. You can't blame somebody else by saying: 'He makes me so angry' or 'She makes me feel so guilty'. You display the emotions, behaviour, and attitude that are inside you already. If you blame somebody else, you are actually dodging your responsibility. In John 14:27, Jesus tells his disciples not to be angered or upset by the world around them. They should not allow other people to dominate them and to make them fearful.

We have a choice. This ability to choose is one of our strongest powers.

Everything that falls outside your territory is out of your control. You are not responsible for it. You can't control other people's behaviour, nor the effect it has on people. For example, Rita can't take responsibility for Klaus's rants and his lack of respect for his family members. She also can't take responsibility for the impact Klaus's behaviour is having on Liezel. She does not control Liezel's reaction to her dad's violent outbursts either. How those two people choose to behave falls outside her territory. She can and should, however, take responsibility for how she allows the devastating effect of her husband's destructive behaviour to continue. She is also responsible to protect her children (physically and emotionally) as best she can.

Rita takes action

Rita has no control over Klaus's choices and behaviour. She does, however, control her reaction to that behaviour. Her decision will have far-reaching consequences for their family. If she chooses to ignore Klaus's behaviour or keep making excuses for it, nobody in the family will benefit, including Klaus. Hopefully, Rita's road to recovery will offer Klaus the opportunity to acknowledge his problem and become accountable.

> ### Redefinition creates room
> ### for re-creation.

For Rita, redefining her identity was a good starting point. To her, the process of rediscovering and celebrating her individuality was challenging, but also liberating. It did cause her anger towards Klaus and herself to increase initially. Klaus's egotism and his lack of respect fell squarely in his territory, not hers. But she had to take responsibility for allowing his destructive behaviour on her piece of land and accepting it for so long. She managed to do that by fixing her fence first.

Just as you do not plant seed on soil that is covered in weeds, but prepare the soil first, so you have to prepare the ground of your heart to receive the seed of God's truth. (Read more about this in Luke 8:4–15 and Matthew 13:3–8.) First, you have to safeguard your territory, and then you have to clear the weeds, plough, and fertilise. Only then the seed of his truth can germinate and take root in your life. Without proper preparation, you will never become the type of person you can be in Him. You will never experience lasting change.

When you develop enough self-respect, you start tilling the soil of your heart to create the room you need to grow to full personhood. Redefinition creates room for re-creation.

Rita reached a point where she could be honest with herself. She confronted her participation in Klaus's mistreatment of her (by allowing it). She realised that Klaus's behaviour and choices were not under her control. But the influence it had was. She had to take responsibility for, and control of, that. Once her worth as a person had been restored, Rita could spell out to Klaus what an acceptable environment for their marriage and family looked like. Thanks to new boundaries, she could look life squarely in the eye. Nobody could manipulate her anymore.

Conclusion

Rita allowed her husband to trespass on her territory and control her choices. To become whole, she first had to cultivate the ground of her heart. A sturdy fence around her territory and a healthy respect for what is hers equipped her to create room for God's truth in her life.

God commands us to love Him with all our heart and all our soul and all our mind. He also commands us to love our neighbour as ourselves (see Matt 27:37–40). Hidden in this command is an important hint about the order in which the love flows. There are three persons that deserve our love: God, our neighbour and ourselves.

Rita had to forgive herself for neglecting her territory. She also had to love herself enough to fix its boundaries and tend the ground inside it.

MEDITATE A MOMENT

- Do you feel as if you're a different person to whom you were before?
- Are there aspects of yourself and your environment that you hide? Are you trying to avoid conflict at any cost? Why?
- What is there in your environment that you would like to change?
- In what ways are you taking responsibility for your emotions, behaviour and attitude?
- Which obstacles in your world are hindering you from moving forward and/or living more fully? Why?

Prayer

*King of my life, thank you that I may also call
you King of my territory.
Thank you for loving me enough that I can be a person in
my own right, and that I am not dependent on other
people's opinion of me.
I only want to see myself in the smooth reflection of your mirror.
Thank you, Father, that I am not a victim of my genes, my past or
the environment. I am in control of my life, and I accept this huge
responsibility in dependence on You.
Help me, Lord, through your Spirit, to discern the things I am
responsible for, as well as the responsibilities I cannot and should
not shoulder. I do not want to keep pretending and allow other
people's choices and sin to hurt me. I do not want my behaviour to
enable them any further. I do not want to allow intruders on my
property anymore. They sow confusion and damage things
I have carefully cultivated. Give me wisdom to
identify and remove every intruder.
Thank you that I am able to tend the soil in
anticipation of the seed of your truth.
I ask this in the Name of your Son, my Saviour, Jesus.
Amen.*

A PRAYER FOR CHANGE

Creator God and Precious Father, I want to put all the conditions and assumptions that permeated my thinking and took me on many rabbit trails behind me. They all, jointly and individually, torpedo my progress and prevent me from moving away from a life of struggle to a life that works, a life of wisdom and intimacy with You.

I want to live in your presence so that You can be my Teacher. I want to know your heart and convey your love to others. I want to live in harmony with your truth.

I declare my dependence on You for this process of rediscovery and growth. I trust You to lead me on a path of realignment and re-creation. You know that my inner capacity is still limited, Lord. Change me little by little, so that I can grow spiritually fit and have more and more room for your truth.

Thank you that I know that You want to change me through the marvellous redemption that your Son achieved for me.

In the Name of your Son, my Saviour, Jesus.

Amen.

PART 2

WHO WE ARE

Principles that start you
- and keep you -
on the road to victory

When it dawns on you that specific aspects of life will either propel you forward or push you back, you have arrived at an important fork in the road. You know that you may choose, and understand that your choices have consequences. To make a wise choice, you need knowledge about the subject your choice is about. In this case, you need knowledge about *yourself*. You have to know who you are. You have to choose how *you* want to live.

> **You have to run your knowledge through the filter of God's truth.**

Knowledge is a well from which you can draw when you are confronted by choices. However, you have to know whether your knowledge represents truth or whether it is misleading, because the latter will only take you directly to another dead end. When you view knowledge in the light of God's truth, it will enable you to get to where you're supposed to be. You have to run your knowledge through the filter of God's truth. Then you will no longer be boxed in by your choices. Instead, they will mobilise you with fresh momentum. Your behaviour will start to reflect your new beliefs. Your life will become an open letter to the world about the saving grace of Jesus (see Philippians 1:27).

How can you be sure that your knowledge reflects God's truth about life in general and your life in particular? That is what we will explore in Part 2.

CHAPTER 7

IDENTITY

Celebrate your
birthright

For me, coffee shops carry a lot of good memories. My dad and I used to frequent them, and we would have interesting discussions about anything and everything. When a topic excited him, he would grab a paper serviette and capture his philosophical musings on it. He also wrote notes on the paper coaster that came with the coffee cup. He would write down the date, what the weather was like, and then pen a short note of endearment to a loved one who could not be there. I treasure my collection of coffee shop notes to this day.

My dad always spoke about someone's '-ness' when he referred to the particular qualities that set someone apart – the way people conduct themselves and how they treat people. Your -ness reveals your uniqueness. It is what others see when you enter a room. It is almost like your character's fingerprint. It is the energy that helps you to create the atmosphere you carry with you.

> **Your past leaves indelible footprints in your soul. Fortunately, you decide where those footprints ultimately lead.**

All of us carry our specific atmosphere, vibe or -ness with us. My dad's vibe was upbeat, sincere and positive. He always exuded an abundant zest for life. It was contagious.

Your story and *your* choices

People are precious. Every person has a unique story to tell, our own share of history. We all have baggage to carry too, all the personal stuff from our past that we bring with us. A lot of us pretend that our baggage does not exist. We try to bury it, or at least to hide it where no one can find it – ourselves included. However, the effort drains a lot of our energy, much to our own detriment and that of our loved ones. The only way to avoid emotional and spiritual exhaustion is to pause next to your baggage and become a 'baggage handler'.

> **You control your interpretations,
> your choices, and the impact
> of the past on you.**

William, the man with the short fuse in Chapter 2, illustrates the importance of such reflection. He had to open the suitcase of the past to analyse and handle his burdens one by one before he could become the man his wife and child needed. The same goes for Michelle in Chapter 5. She had to review her relationship with her mother and her sister before she could see herself in the light of God's truth.

Your past matters, because it leaves indelible footprints in your soul. Fortunately, you can decide where those footprints will ultimately lead. Sometimes, the things that happened in your past are buried so deep that it requires a lot of excavating. It might also involve consulting other people about, for example, your time in the womb, your birth and your childhood. These events shape your story in significant ways.

Does that mean that your past holds you hostage? The short answer is: No, definitely not. The impact of past experience on the present and on your future lies in *your* hands. It falls within your purview, your territory. You control your interpretations and your choices.

You also control the impact of the past on you. The choices that you make determine the direction your life takes.

You are unique.

You are you. One of a kind. Unique in every sense. Your uniqueness lies in your peculiar combination of qualities. No two people share the same combination. Lord Robert Winston, chairman of the Genesis Research Foundation and Professor of Science and Society, puts it this way: 'If my parents want another child with my genes, they need to have another quadrillion (1 with fifteen zeros) babies.'

You are a complex being. No matter how useful categories and classifications are, you are more than the sum of your parts. Every part of you is interwoven with every other part to produce a unique expression of being. We classify people's personality types, but that provides little more than a guideline about your tendencies. At best, it predicts the qualities that will be revealed by most of your actions. However, your personhood remains unique and undefinable, and in that mystery lies a great deal of life's excitement. Furthermore, every person is a dynamic being. We change and we grow, hopefully towards renewal and advancement. Your -ness is not so much seen by others, but perceived by them. You can be unaware of the vibe your presence carries. Still, your interaction with others bears witness to your unique story.

Every person has his or her own unique DNA song.

Your uniqueness lies both in your biological makeup and your non-physical characteristics. Your fingerprint is one of your most unique features. In fact, the fingerprints on your left hand differ from the ones on your right hand, even though they look like mirror images. The iris of your eye, with its unique stripes and gaps that resemble a barcode, also illustrates your uniqueness. Your white blood cells are excellent spies. They can detect which cells in your body are yours and which ones are invaders. Your voice is also uniquely yours. Biometric voice recognition software splits the human voice into a combination of frequencies, each of which is unique, much like your fingerprint.

Hidden in every cell of your body is a wealth of information about your genes. Genetic information resides in two double-stranded helixes. It is called DNA (deoxyribonucleic acid). One of the most interesting aspects of your DNA is its composition. Two polynucleotide strings spiral around each other, like ladders that are twisted around each other. Each rung of the 'ladder' consists of strategically grouped genetic 'letters' (adenine [A], cytosine [C], guanine [G] and thymine [T]). These letters function like codes for a specific arrangement or grouping of amino acids. Amino acids, in turn, are the building blocks of proteins. Later, we shall discuss how information is conveyed by these groupings, because different interpretations of what you see, hear, and experience make up an important part of your re-creation journey.

This spiral with its combinations of four letters also reveals your uniqueness. There is a tune inside you that is as unique as your genetic information. In 2009 a biologist, Dr David Deamer, and a musicologist, Susan Alexjander, measured DNA's molecular vibrations. They determined a sound frequency for each component of DNA. Thus, each individual's unique inner song could be discerned and heard.

Stuart Mitchell became known for his arrangements of DNA music, which he calls 'genome music'. He and his team transfer DNA sound vibrations to musical frequencies and adapt the tempo to real-time. The end result is wonderfully tranquil music with melodies that reflect the unique tune of people's lives.

Every person has his or her own unique DNA song.[1] Your life hums a one-of-a-kind melody. However, the question remains: How harmonious is your inner song?

Disturbing your harmony

What happens when your inner harmony turns into a cacophony, or what if trauma in the womb or negativity by your parents reduces your birth melody to dissonant sounds?

The good news is that discord can be rectified! The road to recovery does require certain inner adjustments, though. Once recovery has taken place, disturbances tend to have a less disruptive effect, and your inner harmony can return to its sweet melody quicker and easier.

People and situations will always try to invade your inner space and destroy your peace. One of the things that usually challenge my inner harmony is dealing with unreasonable people.

It upsets me time after time and causes me to withdraw positive emotion from my emotional account. Other people are irked by indifference, incompetence, or a lack of urgency.

**A feeling of self-worth increases
your capacity to act.**

You were created to thrive on the feel-good energy of others. The state of mind of the people around you always impacts you, whether negatively or positively. Positive people automatically make life more enjoyable for others, while negative, unfriendly people are a drain on those around them. That is what happened to William's family. His story appears in Chapter 2. Klaus's wife and children (Chapter 6) had to bear the brunt of his daily outbursts of anger. The temper and disrespect displayed by men like Klaus and William can either be absorbed by their families, or it can be processed step by step.

The way Klaus behaved was out of his family's control, but how its impact was processed was not. Rita and her children first had to discover their own worth. Their newfound appreciation of their self-worth equipped them to decide on an appropriate reaction to Klaus's behaviour.

A feeling of self-worth acts as an effective buffer or shock absorber to the negative impact of angry people around you. It increases your inner ability (capacity) to act. In the end Klaus was given an ultimatum: Either take responsibility for your behaviour and change, or stand by and watch as your family moves out of your circle of impact.

Somebody who had to make a similar choice was Phillip. Here is his story.

Phillip

It was a balmy autumn afternoon. I do not know where the pharmacist got my number, but as soon as he called, I drove there and made my way to the clinic at the back. A tall, slender, stylishly dressed man sat on the couch with his head tilted backwards and eyes closed, as if he wanted to shut out everything around him.

When I entered, he slowly opened his eyes and looked at me warily.

'Hello,' I said and quietly sat down on the couch next to him.

We moved to the pharmacy's consulting room to talk more privately, and Phillip eventually agreed to see me at the practice the next day.

This middle-aged auditor's life was saved by a quick-thinking pharmacist that Tuesday. His attempt to get hold of prescription medication that would put him to sleep permanently gave away his plan.

Beth and the children came to fetch him while we were still talking. His family led him away, their arms locked in his, like a soft care blanket draped around his shoulders.

Beth accompanied Phillip on his first visit to my consulting room. She sat close to her husband and held his hand the entire time. The worry was clearly etched on her face.

'Phillip doesn't want to be here,' she said tiredly. She sighed, signalling a long battle to get her husband to be whole.

'Why, Phillip?' I had to draw a reaction from him.

For the rest of the appointment, Phillip shared his life story haltingly and brokenly. Every now and then he would close his eyes, because certain parts of the story were not easy to tell. The pain of his childhood left him deeply scarred. There were quite a few incidents about which Beth was blissfully unaware. That Wednesday she was inducted into the world of someone she thought she knew well, but who proved otherwise.

Although Phillip was brilliant at his job, sometimes his anxiety was so bad that he purposely forgot about meetings. Over the years he had built up a solid client base, and he was committed to delivering excellent work. Anxiety and the dark cloud of depression increasingly started to undermine his work ethic. Phillip gave up on the idea of ever receiving any relief.

> **Traumatic experiences lie deeper, waiting for us to develop the capacity to face and process them.**

'I feel like the biggest fake. Everybody thinks I'm coping, but meanwhile I'm hiding in the bathroom in a cold sweat.' Phillip covered his face with both his hands. 'I ... I just can't continue like this.' He looked up and looked me straight in the eye. 'I'm not coping with life, Gerdi. I don't think I belong here.'

Beth quietly blew her nose. Up to this point she had only been aware that her husband was unhappy. She was saddened by the revelation of his struggle and anxiety, but she lovingly stroked his arm and assured him that she did not mind. She was *there* for him.

'Actually,' my client said, somewhat unaware of his wife's pain, 'I should never have been born.' He sat back and looked at his hands. For some time, no words passed between us.

'When did you start feeling this way, Phillip?' I gently probed after a while.

My client slowly looked up. His voice sounded tired. 'Ever since I can remember,' he said.

Prenatal memories

Every person's life story is recorded at the very core of our being. Normally, our history lies in the shallows. It is quickly drafted into the rest of our being. However, traumatic experiences lie much deeper, waiting for us to develop the capacity to face and process them. Such experiences are stored away so that we can process the shock little by little, according to our personal capacity to handle confrontation.

Traumatic stories or incidents surrounding one's birth eventually make its way to the surface of our awareness. When these memories start to well up, it is wise to verify them, if possible. Often, clients wonder whether they suffer from an overactive imagination, but in most cases their memories are confirmed as true. Sometimes there is also a measure of denial: People do not want to acknowledge their inner story to be true.

For the longest time, science denied the validity of suppressed memories that surface during therapy. New research has, however, lent weight to these experiences and sparked serious debate about the role of prenatal memories. How is it possible that people can remember events from before their birth? How can an unborn baby encode experiences when it does not possess the language to describe it? How can events be described when they happened before the brain's hippocampus and amygdala had developed?

The almond-shaped part of our brain called the amygdala handles and regulates emotional expression. Along with the hippocampus, it is responsible for forming long-term memories. Is it possible for a baby's experiences in the womb to be captured by something other than the brain?

When newborns hear music that was played by or to their moms before they were born, clear sound recognition responses can be observed. This also happens when they hear their mothers' voices. According to Dr

A CHANGE OF HEART

Arnold Scheibel, everything a mother eats, drinks or feels, as well as the way she interacts with her unborn baby, have a direct impact on the embryo's neural development.

Experts have recorded a good deal of documentation around people's prenatal memories.[2] These incidents simply cannot be explained without the possibility of an invisible means of recording other than the brain. The intensity of the recalled womb incidents is also being investigated. It seems that traumatic events, such as accidents, abuse or birth trauma, are often remembered.

> ## Our lives are no accident.

It is important to keep in mind that merely recalling an incident will not automatically solve your problem. Such incidents likely cause you to have warped perception, believing lies about yourself, others, and God. These perceptions first have to be rectified. A detox of the soul is called for. Only then effective healing can take place. We shall discuss the detox process in detail in the following chapters.

The reason for your birth

The Gospel according to John starts with the following words:

> In the beginning the Word already existed. The Word was with God, and the Word was God. He existed in the beginning with God. God created everything through him, and nothing was created except through him. The Word gave life to everything that was created, and his life brought light to everyone (1:1–5 NLT).

God is the source of all life. He breathes his life (*neshama* in Hebrew) into our bodies, making us a living soul. His life-giving breath is the source of all life. The fact that we were created in God's image holds a revelation for us: Our lives are no accident. Your existence is about much more than the sexual union between two people. After conception, the zygote (fertilised egg) attaches to the uterus wall and starts to develop. Life has been created.

A number of Scripture verses confirm that God knows us even before we are born. To Jeremiah He said:

88

'I knew you before I formed you in your mother's womb. Before you were born I set you apart and appointed you as my prophet to the nations.'

> – JEREMIAH 1:5 NLT

The psalmist sings:

Every day of my life was recorded in your book.

> – PSALM 139:16 NLT

I believe there comes a moment when God breathes life into the fertilised egg. He does not need the biological parents' or donors' permission to do that. Sometimes the pregnancy is morally questionable, inconvenient, or even the consequence of sexual assault. But there comes a time when the Source of life initiates the growth and development of a human, and that is when life begins. Our lives, therefore, cannot be a fluke, a burden or a mistake. It is simply impossible. The Source of life chose to breathe his life into you. You are his choice. Moreover, you have to believe that God created you with a purpose. It can be a liberating discovery with far-reaching implications.

But what was God's purpose in creating you? Why did He make you and place you on earth in a specific place and a specific time? I believe there are primary and secondary reasons. We were primarily created to know Him in the context of a relationship with Him. According to Genesis 1:27–28, God created man to be his image bearers on earth, and to 'reign' over all the living things. That means that people are responsible for creation and that we must look after it. It also means that we should work with our Heavenly Father to bring reconciliation between Him and all people. Paul said:

This means that anyone who belongs to Christ has become a new person. The old life is gone; a new life has begun! And all of this is a gift from God, who brought us back to himself through Christ. And God has given us this task of reconciling people to him.

> – 2 CORINTHIANS 5:17–18 NLT

You are a part of the re-creation work that Jesus accomplished in us through his death and resurrection. That re-creation work has to gain traction in us before we can start spreading it to the rest of the world. When you are changed, it is like a pebble that is dropped in a pond. Your impact is like the ripples that form on the water when the pebble hits. It keeps getting bigger.

The influence you have on your environment often happens through relationships. Reconciliation makes relationship possible. It starts with a restored relationship with our Heavenly Father. The Holy Spirit then uses you to bring reconciliation between God and people, and between people and other people.

This reconciliation is the balm for all the damage that has been wreaked by rejection and other trauma. It involves a makeover that includes all of you, even your DNA. God's re-creation work will inspire you to sing a new inner song. Your inner harmony will become a praise song full of worship and gratitude. At last, you have come home. You can echo David's proclamation: 'The LORD rewarded me for doing right. He has seen my innocence' (Ps 18:24 NLT). Or, as *The Message* paraphrase puts it, 'God rewrote the text of my life when I opened the book of my heart to his eyes.' That is true transformation.

Your Creator God knows you. He made you. He planned you and shaped you. You do not live at the mercy of the message dictated by your genes or your instinct. You change and you build – a future, a system, a solution to your problems. All the while you are reunited more closely with your Creator God.

This truth was pivotal for Phillip on his road to recovery.

What is a person worth?

Every day, Mr Graham, an elderly gent, wakes up and goes out to the front porch of his modest home. Seated in his favourite chair, he smokes his pipe, sips his coffee and stares into the distance at the houses that stretch to the horizon. He does not talk much. He does not do much either. That is pretty much what his day looks like. Every day.

What is Mr Graham's life worth compared to, say, the president of a country like the United States? The answer is simple. Mr Graham and the president's lives are worth the same. Both are people created in the image of God. At one point God breathed his life into both of them so that they may have a relationship with Him.

There is a difference in the impact they make, though. Mr Graham's current lifestyle choices make him a person with low impact, which is regrettable. Despite his age, he could play a significant role in the lives of his children and grandchildren, if he wanted to. But Mr Graham will only increase his impact once he realises his value and recognises the potential locked up inside him. Then he must agree to share his energy and unlock his worth for everyone's benefit.

My husband and I often travel to Oudtshoorn. En route, we like to stop in Robertson, a lovely town with friendly, inspiring people and quaint, interesting shops. One of our regular stops is a coffee shop with an art gallery next door. One day I saw a painting there that practically begged me to buy it. It was not cheap. Not by a long shot. I stood in front of it for a long time, sipping on a coffee to lift my spirits, desperately hoping I had imagined the price. The longer I stood, the more it appealed to me.

> **The discovery of our worth will progress from an inner awareness to outer recognition.**

After weighing the pros and cons and some creative budgeting, I walked into the gallery one Friday afternoon to buy the painting. I left the gallery most satisfied with my new treasure. After careful consideration I had decided that the painting was worth its price. I did not pay too much.

But how much is a person worth? And what is a reasonable price for all of humanity? Even if we do not know it, we too had been 'for sale' at one stage. Fortunately, Someone bought us – at an extremely high price. 'God bought you with a high price,' Paul says in 1 Corinthians 6:20 (NLT). Some two thousand years ago, Jesus paid the full ransom for us, buying our freedom from Satan's kingdom of darkness and despair, and bringing us into his kingdom of truth and light.

Our acceptance of this divine exchange confirms our citizenship of God's kingdom. We become God's children and his heirs. According to Genesis 4:10, blood has a voice – Abel's blood cried out to God. Similarly, the blood of the Lamb of God that was shed on the cross loudly proclaims his love for us! How can we ever doubt our worth?

The discovery of our worth will progress from an inner awareness to outer recognition. When you start understanding your worth and that of others, you will start adjusting your behaviour towards them. And the way others perceive your behaviour and your communication (your

-ness) will change too. The value you attach to yourself and to other people is reflected in your behaviour towards them.

Another by-product of discovering your worth is an increased feeling of gratitude. The greater the value, the deeper the gratitude. Your appreciation and gratitude exude a specific energy, and such a -ness provides pleasure to those around you.

Your self-worth affects your behaviour:

Low self-worth – flippant behaviour
High self-worth – respectful behaviour

Understanding your considerable self-worth changes all your relationships – with other people, with God, and with yourself. If you do not acknowledge your worth, you will never claim your birthright. You will never respect yourself. But when respect forms the foundation of your relationships, you create room for courageous honesty.

Michelle, about whom we read in Chapter 5, experienced this first-hand. Her very first relationship, the one with her mother, was based on fear. She did not understand what love was, and therefore struggled to love herself. She felt embittered and angry. She did not know how to have successful relationships with herself and others. I am very grateful that she chose to replace fear with love. It was hard work, but it made a lasting difference in her and Peter's life.

Love and respect always go together; the one cannot exist without the other. We should examine these two aspects of our relationships regularly. When you know your self-worth and respect yourself, you can build meaningful relationships with other people.

If, however, you develop a fake identity for the sake of maintaining 'peace', you sacrifice your entire birthright. Rita lost her identity little by little in a desperate attempt to create harmony in the home. She kept on accommodating Klaus's lack of respect towards her, which robbed her of self-respect. In the process, she developed a codependent personality. Rita represents an enormous percentage of humanity. A codependent personality develops when your image or definition of yourself keeps adjusting in the hopes of pleasing significant people in your life. However, you are just accommodating their sinful behaviour. It is a lose-lose situation. Such behaviour fails to prompt change in the guilty party. On the contrary, you lose your self-worth and reinforce the other person's abusive behaviour.

Your bowl of lentil stew

Like Esau in the Bible, you can also lose or trade your birthright. Most often it happens subconsciously, leaving you aimless and confused, or it can drive you to thoughts of self-harm, like Phillip.

You receive your birthright certificate even before you are born: *I have a God-given right to be here. My lungs are filled with the breath of the Holy Spirit.*

You run the risk of losing your birthright due to trauma and illegitimate claims. Intimidation, domination, and manipulation by others (gaslighting) can lead to confusion and self-doubt. Rejection by loved ones can hurt you to the point of giving up your birthright. Situations will often leave you with unfair, even impossible choices. Then your most basic right, your birthright, is stolen, robbing you of the power to choose.

If you are unaware of your birthright, and if authority figures keep undermining you, you will forever wrestle with the hows and whys of your existence. You will, despite repeated efforts, never manage to believe that you are worth the gift of life that has been granted to you. Phillip tried his whole life to convince himself of his worth, and also to convince his mother, the primary figure of his childhood, that his existence was justified. Over time, Phillip (with Beth close by his side) and I started to dig ever deeper, going back further into the past. The main avenue that we explored was his firm conviction that he should never have been born. I asked him why he had been plagued by suicidal thoughts his whole life. He remembered feeling the pull of death even as a young boy.

'What was your birth like, Phillip?' I asked when we were together again one winter's morning.

'I have no idea. I suppose it was OK.'

Of course, that was his own take on events. The other participants in what had transpired were not there, so we continued coming up against Phillip's one-sided perspective. I wanted to know whether there were complications during birth, and/or whether his life had even been endangered before or during birth. Without sharing this hunch with him or Beth, I encouraged him to have a talk with his mother. He duly approached her and asked her about her pregnancy and his birth. As it turns out, that conversation and the following session proved to be vital to his recovery.

'She didn't want me,' Phillip said. He was devoid of emotion, at least initially, as if he was merely relaying something inconsequential. The wall around his heart was still standing, but the foundations were wobbling. That was not all Phillip had heard from his mom. What she said, finally shed some light on his preoccupation with death as a solution.

Phillip's mom had tried to abort him. She simply did not want another baby, since her two older children had reached the stage where she could continue pursuing her career. Her do-it-yourself attempt had been unsuccessful, but she did enough to invite death into her child's life, as it were. Her effort had made an indelible impression on the little baby in the womb. It was not Phillip's doing. The authority figure in his life had made a pact with death. Therefore, it kept on calling to him, and it would continue calling until either Phillip or his mom complied with the agreement, or until it was consciously terminated by him in his adult capacity.

His traumatic experience in the womb left my client with a firm belief that he was better off dead. His birthright was stolen from him even before his birth.

The walls Phillip had erected for his own safety would have to be broken down before he could strike out on a new path in the light of God's truth. He could reclaim his birthright in the knowledge that it legitimately belonged to him. The value God attached to him was fixed and certain. Phillip merely had to realise and accept it.

Phillip takes action

'Who is Phillip?' I asked after that breakthrough session. This simple question stumps the majority of my clients, at least for a moment.

'Uhm … I don't know,' he said hesitantly after a brief silence.

In order to grow to maturity and to be reconciled with yourself and your Saviour, you have to realise that you have permission to be on earth. Acknowledging this makes the question about identity a vital one to answer.

For the first time, Phillip gave himself permission to live. Subsequently, he had to find out who it was he gave permission to. His inward journey led him to discover and acknowledge all the good and praiseworthy aspects of his -ness. He had to accept the strengths, but also the weaknesses that formed part of his identity. Some of his weaknesses were things he could work on; others he had to accept as part of his human fallibility.

We gradually started working on his anxiety disorder, and his new definition of who he was further equipped him to deal with inner conflict. At this stage, in light of his new truth, he was able to identify his underlying fear much easier. Phillip could act proactively to handle his anxiety, which further bolstered his sense of self-worth.

This gentle soul's biggest breakthrough came as he enthusiastically opened himself to life and claimed his birthright. The day he declared with conviction: 'I have a God-given right to be here! I *want* to be here! I choose life!' was a red-letter day for their family.

Phillip patiently worked through the process of forgiving his mom, his dad and himself. He had to 'forgive' his Heavenly Father too. He resented God for allowing him to be born but denying him an abundant life (so he thought). Step by step his thoughts had to be aligned with the new reality (his new belief) that he had *permission* to be here, because he carried the very breath of God in his lungs.

To me, Phillip and every person who ever worked through similar issues, are champions through and through.

Conclusion

An inheritance is not awarded on the grounds of merit or qualification. Heirs can enjoy their inheritance or live as if they never received it. If you want to use your divine inheritance, you first have to realise that you inherited it. Only then can you claim your inheritance and gradually incorporate its impact into your life. You will also have to continuously protect your precious inheritance, not only for your own sake, but also for the glory of Him who granted you such a big gift of grace.

In the next chapters, we shall discuss accepting, protecting, and maintaining your divine inheritance. The depth of your gratitude and the sense of responsibility you feel as a result of it, determine to which extent you will live a victorious life. That, in turn, determines whether your impact will have eternal value.

MEDITATE A MOMENT

1. Do you believe that you have a God-given right to live? Do you acknowledge your birthright?
2. What excites you?
3. Which activities (daily or weekly) energise you?
4. Which activities drain you?
5. What do you excel at? (It's fine to repeat them if you have mentioned them already.)
6. Which activities do you avoid because you struggle with them?
7. About which aspect of your life do you feel ashamed?
8. What are the aspects you can work on? Which ones should you accept as is?
9. When you are ready, please proclaim the following over yourself:
- I declare that I have the right to live and to enjoy life to its fullest.
- I declare that I accept my whole being, not just my strengths or good attributes, but also not just my weaknesses and shortcomings. I now embrace all aspects of my personality without regret, blame, or rejection.
- I declare that I no longer want to hide my weaknesses from others for fear of criticism, ridicule, or rejection.
- I also declare that I want to maintain a good relationship with myself, because self-respect is a requirement for my state of mind, my health, and my future. This relationship will echo in eternity.
- Self-acceptance is like a launchpad I use to accurately propel myself towards my calling.

Prayer

*Heavenly Father, thank you that You have always cared for me,
even before I was born. Thank you for choosing to breathe your life
into me. You ransomed me from the kingdom of darkness and
despair through the finished work of Jesus Christ on the cross.
You made a way for me to be reconciled with You, and to
be a legitimate member of your Kingdom.
My sin no longer stands in the way of that reconciliation. When I
bring my lack of belief and obedience to You, the precious blood of
your Son washes away my sin and makes my life pure,
so that I may live in your presence.
You want to have a relationship with me, because You love me.
I want to be part of your Body. Today I claim my birthright
in the Name of your Son, Jesus my Saviour.
I understand that my life will have an impact when I belong to
You. I believe that You purposely and lovingly created me the way
I am. I believe that You want to reconcile me to You, and that You
want to use my life to reconcile others to You as well. My identity
remains dynamic as I adapt to the plans and the seasons you
determine. I want to form part of your plan – locally and globally!
Today is a day of celebration. Today I celebrate
my birthright with You!
Amen.*

CHAPTER 8

COMPOSITION

Know **yourself**

The lump of soft clay lies in the maker's hands. His strong fingers compress it, knead it, and then start shaping it. Slowly but surely, he brings the dream in his heart to life before the eyes of others. He knows exactly what he wants to make, and he trusts the connection between his hand and his heart.

Your Maker is the God of Israel, the Covenant God of Abraham, Isaac, and Jacob. He is the One who created everything. He, the Source of all life who existed from time immemorial, carried you in his heart. Since long before your birth, He wanted to have a relationship with you, an ordinary person.

He personally established a road to reconciliation with Him for you. The only person who can sabotage that reconciliation is you. He gave you the power to choose. How will you handle such a big responsibility?

Better understanding, better choices

My husband often says: 'No one is as uninformed as the man who does not know that he does not know.' One of the best qualities a person can have, is a hunger for knowledge, a desire to learn and discover. A studious attitude is a prerequisite for enrichment and positive growth.

Knowledge gives you more opportunities to grow. The wider your knowledge of a situation, the better your chances of interpreting and processing the information correctly and making wise choices. It is also important to be well informed concerning your life and effectiveness. Knowledge enables you to have a deep and richly textured relationship with your Father and Saviour. Knowledge opens the door to understanding.

In Part 1, we saw how people's attempts to become whole failed, and how they repeatedly ended up on the wrong track. They all put their focus on a specific aspect of their being. They tried to 'fix' either their body, their mind, or their spirit in order to live a happy, fulfilled life. Unfortunately, their efforts only left them more frustrated and exhausted. They confirmed the American author Ellen Glasgow's words: 'All change is not growth, as all movement is not forward.'

We are more than a body, a soul, or a spirit. We are put together in such a way that each aspect of our being has an area of responsibility. We can only express our true nature and reach our potential to the extent that we understand – and eventually implement – these responsibilities.

You must know how everything fits together. It is important, therefore, that we study our composition as humans, so that we understand the value and function of each aspect. This will help you to align yourself with God's truth and to become whole. It unlocks positive, long-term change.

The term 'monism' is very old, first coined by the German philosopher Christian von Wolff in 1728. Philosophers and scientists started using the term to describe how they viewed people and to explain abnormal behaviour. The term 'mono' means 'one' or 'single'. According to monism, reality only consists of one element – the material world. The theory discounts aspects like the spirit. The only reality is what we can perceive through the five senses. This philosophy does not make a distinction between God and creation.

We are fascinating, living beings with a body and a spirit.

This view has permeated modern neuroscience, which sees a person as a body only. Emotions, thoughts, and reasoning are reduced to brain functions, specifically the electrochemical functioning of the neurons. This viewpoint supports the theory of evolution and natural selection. School textbooks are usually saturated with monistic concepts.

However, monism is not the only theory dreamed up by man. The famous words of French philosopher René Descartes, 'I think, therefore I am,' acknowledge another dimension of humanity. In the sixteenth century, Descartes suggested that human nature consists of the visible world of the physical body as well as people's invisible thoughts.

Inside your thoughts and thinking patterns lies a wealth of complex processes and interpretations. In the twentieth century, the philosopher and neurobiologist John Eccles brought the concept of dualism back as an alternative theory of a person's composition. Dualism works with two opposites – for example, material reality vs. invisible consciousness. Eccles received a Nobel Prize for his research on the brain. To Eccles, optical illusions and the fact that one picture could have more than one interpretation (see illustration below) indicated that there had to be something more than merely the physical brain. Something other than the brain contributes to the individual's interpretation. He made the following important statement: 'Naturalism fails to account for our experienced uniqueness … I am constrained to attribute the uniqueness of the Self or Soul to a supernatural spiritual creation.'

Do you see a young girl or an old woman? This sketch and similar ones proved to neurobiologist John Eccles that people have a psychological component, which causes them to interpret things differently.

There is a third theory about people's composition. Many scientists feel that monism and dualism are incomplete. A person is more than physical, and even more than the dualistic view of body and thoughts. Mario Beau-regard and Denyse O'Leary[1] promote the view that a person is also a spiritual being.

Their research about religious experience (sometimes called reli-gious-spiritual mystic experiences) refers to people's connection to something outside the material world.

Einstein formulated it as follows: 'The most beautiful emotion we can experience is the mystical. It is the power of all true art and science. He to whom this emotion is a stranger, who can no longer wonder and stand rapt in awe, is as good as dead.'

As a Christian, I believe that God created us remarkable and intricate. He definitely did not limit us to a body with emotions and thoughts. We are fascinating, living beings with a body and a spirit. These aspects of ours are often mentioned in God's Word. They are inseparably intertwined and interdependent. Paul's prayer for the church in Thessalonica refers to this:

> Now may the God of peace make you holy in every way, and may your whole spirit and soul and body be kept blameless until our Lord Jesus Christ comes again.
>
> – 1 THESSALONIANS 5:23 NLT

The position, responsibility, and especially the hierarchy of each of these aspects of our being are vitally important in our definition of who we are. It is also important for us to lead effective lives. When one investigates this topic in God's Word, you find hundreds of references to a person's body, soul, thoughts, will, emotions, and spirit as they relate to their function.

The Bible contains more than 900 references[2] to a person's heart:

- In Proverbs 4:23 we read: 'Guard your heart above all else, for it de-termines the course of your life' (NLT).
- Proverbs 23:7 declares: 'For as he thinks in his heart, so *is* he.'
- In 1 Peter 3:4, Peter writes about 'the hidden person of the heart'.
- And Proverbs 3:3 teaches us: 'Never let loyalty and kindness leave you! Tie them around your neck as a reminder. Write them deep within your heart' (NLT).

The Hebrew word for 'heart' is leḇ or lēḇāḇ (pronunciation: lev or le-vav), which means 'the innermost organ'. The root word lēḇāḇ means 'the entire disposition of the inner person'. A person's heart is the seat of his or her being. It is here that change needs to take place if a person truly wants to live a new life.

According to Scripture, a person is a living being, a soul, who has a body, heart, and spirit. Each of these aspects has a special position and function. If we understand each one's position and function, we will make more effective decisions and function more effectively. Let's do a brief overview of the different aspects of the self.

According to Scripture, man:
1. Was created by God – in his likeness, male and female.
2. Was created as a body from the dust of the ground.
3. Received his spirit through the living energy of God's divine breath, the Spirit of Life.
4. Became a living being, a soul, as God breathed life into his physical body.

In Scripture, the three words used for 'life' are:
1. zōé – eternal, divine life (John 10:10)
2. bíos – physical life (Luke 8:14)
3. psuché – soul-life, a living, breathing creature (Matt 16:25)

You do not *have* a soul; you *are* a soul. You are a living creature who can love your Creator with all of your soul – i.e. with your whole being. In other words, soul is not just an aspect of the self, but a collective noun for all the aspects that make you human.

The body

The body is part of the visible self. The body links the invisible part of you to the rest of your environment and often acts as the go-between between your subconscious and your conscious self. When your body becomes sick, you should keep in mind that the cause sometimes lies deeper, so you should devote time to the invisible aspect of your being as well.

The body's biggest question is: *How will this situation affect my survival?*

The spirit

The spirit is an invisible part of the self. Your spirit connects you to the invisible spirit realm. Your spirit connects you either to God's kingdom or Satan's kingdom. It can happen consciously or subconsciously – the latter especially when you are ignorant or choose to be.

The spirit's biggest questions are: *Who is my god?* or *How will this situation affect my faith or moral view?*

The heart

The heart is the deepest part of one's identity, and the aspect of self that ranks highest. Your heart carries your convictions and your truth, that often differs from God's truth. Your truth is based mainly on your experiences, your interpretation of your experiences, and the disposition you are born with.

Your uniqueness lies in who your heart believes you are. With your heart you form your self-definition, your truth, beliefs, relationships, behaviour, and the atmosphere around you.

Your heart connects the physical with the spiritual (body with spirit). You communicate with yourself and others through your emotions, mind, and behaviour. We shall discuss this in greater detail later.

The heart's biggest questions are: *Who am I? How will this situation affect my self-definition?*

Mariele

Mariele struggled back to her dormitory after dark, in the pouring rain. She had stopped wiping away her tears, because the rain was soaking her face anyway. She hoped her dorm mates would think it was the storm that had made such a mess of her hair and her clothes.

The first-year student was unaware, however, of just how visible the shock in her eyes was, and that everybody would know that not even a storm could leave her so dishevelled.

'Good heavens, Mariele!' her roommate cried. 'What happened to you?'

Her friends quickly gathered around her.

The rest of her student life was an exhausting struggle to get her degree amidst a plethora of consultations with attorneys and a drawn-out legal battle. Apparently, proving that you have been raped is not that easy, especially if you are an attractive girl, and if the rapist's father is an influential businessman. She completed her degree (eventually, after an extra year) and started work at a small firm close to her parents. Their support carried her. Both parents were dedicated to her recovery all the way. She strived to keep her life manageable and predictable, even boring. She had had enough of risk and stimulation.

Mariele took the scatter cushions on the couch in my consulting room and put them on the carpet, trying to make herself comfortable. More than ten years had passed since her student days already, but the hurt of that period in her life was still woven into her being. She only showed emotion once while telling her story. It was as if she was doing a book report – she was merely conveying facts.

'I'm not here to talk about my "past life". I'm just mentioning these things to give you background. It is bound to crop up sometime, so now you know,' she explained. 'Actually, I'm here about my weight.'

'What is it about your weight that you would like to discuss?' I asked.

She shifted in her seat and made sure that her cellphone's sound was off, again. Then she answered, somewhat annoyed: 'I am fat, and I can't shake off my excess weight. You must help me.'

She was not looking at me, and I noticed the shame behind her curt attitude. She desperately wanted someone to relieve her on the battlefield so that she could get a short reprieve from the fighting. But it was *her* life. She had to live it. I could only come alongside her and help her to avoid the worst pitfalls and obstacles, where possible.

A person's body is a delicate and highly specialised organism.

Fortunately, Mariele pushed through and eventually recovered her original beauty. Even though the road was bumpy and full of potholes, she steadfastly attended therapy until she was comfortable enough to share the couch with all the cushions. Her path gradually led her to self-knowledge.

Our bodies

Your body is an extensive repository of data. It contains more or less 3 billion genetic letters per genome. The body has a very sophisticated air conditioning and filtration system. On average, the heart beats around 100 000 times per day to pump 7 000 litres of blood through 2 500 kilometres of blood vessels.

Even within cells there are hidden surprises that attest to our impressive design. The mitochondrion, an organelle, is a good example. (An organelle is a specialised structure inside our cells that performs a specific function.) Recent research reveals that dysfunctional mitochondria likely play a role in the development of Alzheimer's disease. Another fascinating fact about this 'little organ' is that the dad's mitochondrion is lost during conception, since it is located in the sperm's tail, which falls off after fertilisation. Since the mitochondrion is the only organelle enjoying its very own DNA, the mitochondrial DNA, it is therefore the mother's mitochondria and mitochondrial DNA that are transferred from generation to generation. Scientists even refer to this as the Mitochondrial Eve. Your cells therefore contain archival data on all your female ancestors.

The mitochondria determine when apoptosis should take place. Apoptosis is the programming of cell death to avoid tumour growth.

> **The body often makes known that which lies deeper, in the spirit and the heart.**

A person's body is a delicate and highly specialised organism. It is as if God let his enormous creativity run free when he created man.

The body's role in your life

The body is the tangible, visible part of the self. When one understands the body's role and hierarchy in the self, you can designate it its proper place. The body can be likened to an army's foot soldiers. Even though they occupy the lowest rung, no army can survive without them.

The body simply cannot occupy the highest position or enjoy the highest priority in any definition of self. That is a recipe for imbalance and chaos. Despite this, the body clamours for ascendancy, especially in our society with its materialistic, superficial views and its incessant demands that we should conform to our environment.

If God created our bodies, which are low in the pecking order, with so much wonderful complexity, just imagine what He did with all our other aspects! It would be sad if one devoted more time, energy and money to your appearance and your body's needs than to the other, invisible parts of you. On the other hand, you cannot ignore your body's role and responsibility. Your body receives information through its five senses and connects you to your environment. A person filters almost 99% of this information, but the things you hear, see, taste, smell, and feel still provide you with enough data to make temporary choices. However, it is your psyche (invisible aspects of the self) that interprets all the data and determines your reaction. An aspect of the self other than the visible, material body makes these choices. However, these choices become visible through your body.

Sensory data
+ interpretation (via behavioural patterns and intuition)
= behaviour

One of the body's most important functions is to 'translate' your inner dialogue for your consciousness. For example, when you keep ignoring your inner hurt, your immune system will start acting up. The body often makes known that which lies deeper, in the spirit and the heart. The headaches that Michelle experienced were a cry for help, a plea to pay attention to her struggle with self-acceptance. Fortunately, she acted on it and also started to look for the real root of the problem. Mariele's body rebelled against past injustice. She had to decide to search her spirit for the deeper causes of her physical problems. Spiritual healing led to physical healing.

The different aspects of the self influence each other. Your emotions and thoughts sometimes influence your digestion. By the same token, the food you eat and the liquids you drink can influence your mood and focus. The correlation between emotional problems, diseases, and the digestive system is something that keeps researchers increasingly busy.

As long as you see different aspects of the self separate from each other, you cannot function effectively.

Few things illustrate the relationship between the seen and the unseen as well as the interaction between our nervous system and the digestive tract.

The second brain

Few people are aware that we actually have more than one brain. The nervous system in your intestine, known as the enteric nervous system (ENS), is an independent, self-regulating nervous system located in the wall of the digestive tract. It functions independently of the brain and consists of two thin layers of nerve cells (neurons) that service your intestine from your oesophagus to your rectum. It is approximately 9 meters long. It is not capable of reason and higher cognitive functions, therefore it is sometimes called the second brain.

Thanks to the work of Professor Xiling Shen, a biomedical engineering expert, it is now possible to watch the neurons of nerve cells in the ENS. This part of our autonomous nervous system contains 500 million neurons and five times more neurotransmitters (chemical 'messengers') than the spine.

The central nervous system communicates with the intestine and also determines the speed at which food moves through the intestine, the amount of acid that is secreted, and the mucus production on the lining of the intestine.

Almost 90% of the fibres in the primary intestinal nerve, the vagal nerve, carries information to the brain, not just from the brain. They are the reason we feel tension, excitement or anxiety in the pit of the stomach. At least seven types of serotonin receptors reside in the intestine. In fact, some 95% of the body's serotonin centres in the intestine.

Chronic stress impedes the vagal nerve's function to regulate calmness and focus, a task of the parasympathetic nervous system. High levels of cortisol and adrenaline support the activity of the sympathetic nervous system, keeping the individual on high alert. This may cause emotional congruency and resilience to malfunction, as we will learn later.

Furthermore, there are two specific types of sensory neurons that are constantly checking your intestine. One of them notices when the stomach reckons that the other is reacting to the presence of incoming nutrients. Researchers also discovered that, if a specific probiotic bacteria of the intestine *(Lactobacillus reuteri)* occur in breast milk, it helps to produce oxytocin (our social hormone). This increase in oxytocin takes place via the vagal nerve, which offers further proof of the intestine's (or gut-brain's) impact on the rest of your being, as oxytocin helps one to form positive connections to others.

Trauma has to be handled on a bodily level as well.

Although reasoning and other thought processes fall outside the gut-brain's ambit, it definitely influences your mood. At the moment, research is being done on the correlation between certain moods and the functioning of the ENS, diet, and digestion. It would seem that my client Frieda, whose plan was to straighten out her life through exercise, diet, and medication, was not completely off the mark. Her depression and anxiety were clear indicators of the interaction between brain and intestine. Mariele, too, had to realise the important role of a healthy body in happiness and wholeness. As her knowledge of the subject grew, she developed renewed respect for her body and started to treat it accordingly. Her trauma had to be handled on a bodily level as well.

Bidirectional communication pathways have been identified between the enteric nervous system (ENS), the hypothalamic pituitary adrenal (HPA) axis, the autonomic nervous system (ANS), and the central nervous system (CNS).

These systems, along with the functioning of brain-derived neurotrophic factor (BDNF, see Chapter 3), are highly dependent on the health of your gut microbiota's genome (microbiome). According to estimates by psychotherapist and author Matthew Dahlitz, the gut microbes outnumber the cells in your body by a factor of 10!

This recent discovery confirms the interconnectedness of your gut and brain, and how stressors can affect your mind, your emotions, and your health.

When life throws you a curveball, it influences your gut bacteria. The epithelial gut lining can become more permeable, which allows bacteria to have access across the lining. This can increase metabolic problems and place a higher demand on your immune system in general.

Fight or flight

When Mariele was raped on that rainy evening, her whole being went into a state of shock. She heard and felt the alarms going off inside her, and for a long time faced the unprocessed shock. when she looked in the mirror. Trauma does not necessarily lead to weight problems, but in Mariele's case it did. The trauma of her rape wounded her so deep internally that her body sought a way to make the wounds visible.

> **High stress cannot be eliminated sufficiently without oxytocin.**

When you experience trauma, a fight-or-flight cycle kicks in that is caused by the hypothalamic pituitary adrenal (HPA) axis. This reaction is activated as soon as your senses tell you that you are in danger. The message of impending danger is sent to the hypothalamus in the brain, which instructs the body to release more adrenalin. The pituitary gland obliges. Increased adrenalin causes a raised heartbeat, higher blood pressure and body temperature, sharpened focus, and even extraordinary speed, if needed. The idea behind the fight-or-flight cycle is to get you to safety.

The stress hormone, cortisol, is released and the hippocampus in the brain decides what the best option would be to get you to react quickly. Are you out of harm's way? Can you start relaxing, or are there more situations on the way? Once the danger is over, oxytocin (the social hormone) starts to regulate cortisol levels so that you can relax.

Recent research shows that parenting styles influence genes in children's hippocampuses, as well as the functioning of their HPA axis. It was found that a parenting style which makes children feel secure (unconditional acceptance) leads to changes in genetic expressions, equipping the hippocampus to regulate stress hormones (such as cortisol) effectively. In contrast, households with high stress levels and conditional parenting will negatively impact the hippocampus and the functioning of oxytocin. Parenting is conditional when a parent only demonstrates affection when the child pleases the parent in some way, e.g. by behaving well or doing well at school.

Research[3] further indicates that oxytocin plays a part in empathy during the interpretation of facial expressions, and it confirms that the production of oxytocin has a direct impact on children's ability to build healthy relationships and to be attentive to other peoples' emotional state.

High stress cannot be eliminated sufficiently without oxytocin. Without oxytocin, the fight-or-flight cycle remains active, and stress levels remain high. This is not healthy for any part of you. When children grow up in such a house, they later, as adults, struggle to handle stress effectively by completing the fight-or-flight cycle following a stressful experience. Stress levels remain high, and the person never gets to rest. Soon, they do not know how to relax.

If your HPA axis is active all the time, it not only desensitises you to adrenalin, but it weakens your immune system so that you are constantly being exposed to new crises. It is clear that the visible and invisible aspects of our personality cannot, and should not, be separated. If you do not understand and respect that, the consequences will eventually overtake you.

The feeling, thinking man

You are a being that feels, forms relationships, thinks, and reasons. In the next chapter, we will discuss where these subordinate aspects fit in, and what their roles and functions are.

People were created to cultivate relationships with one another. A child would rather have negative attention from a parent than no attention. A big part of our self-definition is determined by how we see ourselves in relationship with others. In turn, our ability to have relationships with others is determined by our relationship with ourselves.

> Forming strong ties of love with ourselves
> is a precondition for forming true ties
> of love with others.

Our whole being is involved when we form ties with others, but it originates in the heart. These ties can either be constructive, building us up, or destructive and misleading. When we build relationships with others, we invite them in. We make ourselves vulnerable and trust that the outcome will contribute to our quality of life. Unfortunately, that is not always the case. Sometimes the outcome of our connections is so negative that our health has to make itself heard in the hopes that we will disentangle ourselves from the situation.

We form our first relationship ties in the womb already, and all our subsequent relationships are subconsciously measured by that first important relationship. The bond between mother and infant is the most important bond. It enables children to start loving themselves. The more we love and accept ourselves, the more we are able to build relationships with others. Self-rejection impedes our ability to process negative experiences, successfully manage ourselves, and have a positive impact on our environment. Forming strong ties of love with ourselves is a precondition for forming true ties of love with others.

Initially, Mariele's ties with herself, her parents, and her friends were strong. However, being raped not only stole her innocence, but her inner harmony and the expression of her birthright and her calling. She lost perspective, and her body's discomfort brought her inner chaos to the surface.

Your will: the go-between

I will. Willpower will get you far. Your will executes your decisions. It is the connection between your inner management's decisions and your body's actions.

When you start discovering your will as a baby, the respect and loving guidance of your primary caregivers are extremely important. They enable you to gradually learn how powerful – and even dangerous – your will can be. In the beginning, children are taught right and wrong. They are not born with this knowledge, and therefore have to be led – respectfully – to acquire this knowledge. The learning process that the child goes through should, in time, lead them to the point where they follow their own convictions. That is one of the most important responsibilities of a parent. From early on, the child learns that their actions, 'doing' their decisions, have consequences, and that they should carefully consider. That is how the child ultimately learns responsibility and self-control.

> **Your interpretation of events become your truth and even your identity.**

Between your thoughts and your behaviour, the finisher – your will – stands. Your will is supposed to implement your reasoning and decision-making. If you do not know what your components are and how they're put together, prepare for your will to vacillate between the body on the one hand, and thoughts or emotions on the other. A confused will is easily frustrated and exhausted, leading to a loss of willpower, hope and energy.

People are supposed to function with a certain inner regimen. But what if that regimen descends into chaos as a result of bad parenting or other forms of trauma? If you want to re-establish order, you have to restore each aspect of your being to its original role and rank.

Mariele's will was clearly sick and tired after fighting her hurt for so long. Her will had been weakened to the point of giving up. Mariele's will had surrendered its function and role. But something else was also brewing inside her.

Mental tug of war can be exhausting

Deep in the core of Mariele's being reside her heart's convictions. *Her truth, the one determining her whole being, is written on the tablet of her heart.* She dictated it herself when her naivety and innocence were ripped from her that dark, brooding night.

Experiences tattoo themselves on your soul – the more intense the experience, the deeper its influence on who you are. These tattoos soon become your new truth, convictions with the ability to radically alter your self-definition and your decisions. The experiences themselves do not form the truth, but their effect on you does. Your interpretation of the events becomes your new truth and even your identity. If an experience challenges your identity and self-image, your inner reality creates new convictions that fit the interpretation of that experience.

For example, Mariele was happy with her appearance when she was in high school. As a top matric student, she easily qualified for a spot in the dormitory. She started her classes without a care in the world and enjoyed student life with her friends. She was a beautiful young person with a zest for life and positive self-regard. The picture she had of herself was attractive. Then she met Tom, a young man with loads of charm and intense, blue eyes. Unfortunately, his charm evaporated when he turned into a rapist and forced himself on her. His complete lack of respect shattered her healthy self-image into a thousand pieces. Following the incident, Mariele did not think she was attractive anymore. Neither did she want to be. It was as if her appearance somehow gave men permission to humiliate her, and she had no desire to live through another 'misunderstanding' like that.

Her interpretation of the event engraved a new truth on her heart. *As long as I am beautiful, this trauma will repeat itself.* Mariele's will took this new conviction (new truth) and set the wheels in motion. Eating became a means of escape. She made a pact with food. Her new ally became kind of a shield that would protect her against future hurt, or so Mariele thought. The rational Mariele pushed back, however, especially when she stood in front of the mirror or socialised with her friends. Then her mind would give her all the reasons why dieting and exercise were not the worst ideas. After that, her will tried very hard to implement her mind's choices, but her emotions and heart demanded attention and obedience too.

This mental tug of war left her devoid of willpower and wholesome discipline. Her will bowed out and Mariele started to neglect her body. She gave up completely – she wanted other people to handle her problems and even to make decisions on her behalf. Even visiting me was the result of an appointment she had made because her mom had insisted.

'See if she can't help you,' her mom had suggested desperately. I could if she *wanted* to.

Mariele takes action

Convictions make themselves known in different ways. Our behaviour, words, and especially our attitude reveal our personal truth.

One morning while Mariele and I were talking, she told me for the umpteenth time what had happened to her that night. By now, her emotions were fully integrated into her narration. When she talked about the day after, when she had to supply affidavits, she broke down when she mentioned Tom's name. Her tears flowed freely.

'I remember saying to myself: "My life will never be the same again. I am ruined!" when I looked into the mirror the next morning. I did not even want to apply lipstick,' she softly mused.

'Why not?' I asked. It was the first time she had shared this particular nugget.

Mariele grew quieter and closed her eyes. She imagined her younger self standing in front of the mirror in her dormitory room. As she watched young Mariele, she softly said: 'Because then I would look pretty.'

'Stay there, Mariele,' I encouraged. 'Why don't you want to look pretty?'

Her answer hit the nail on the head: 'Because then it can happen again.'

Brave people are the ones who keep going, even when the likely destination will confront them with their biggest fears. Mariele was very brave and did exactly that. When she did, she finally realised that her beauty had not been the catalyst for Tom's behaviour. She also realised that self-neglect did not safeguard her against future assault. She renounced her false convictions and successfully worked through the four steps of change. Her heart could once again appreciate her beauty.

> **Our Maker created us to bring forth
> a wonderful melody.**

If you are not informed about your opinions, your will becomes a slave to your limited knowledge and skewed interpretations. Your will becomes trapped between the competing expectations of the different aspects of your being, and those of others and society. Mariele wanted to farm out her problem to someone else because she could no longer bear to handle her inner conflict. Her will had lost its power. Only when she replaced her truth with God's truth, her will could take its rightful place in her hierarchy and play the role it was supposed to. Mariele's will was freed up to listen only to her heart, without distracting demands from her body, thoughts, and convictions to confuse matters. That strengthened Mariele's self-discipline. Her will chose to love her self again, acting in harmony with her heart.

Conclusion

The Blue Danube is probably the best-known composition by Johann Strauss II. Combined, each instrument's separate contribution brings forth music that fills one with pure joy. How wonderful it would be if our actions also brought forth such an exquisite sound in the invisible realm!

The good news is that it is entirely possible.

Orchestral music moves us when each instrument plays its part accurately. Composition refers to optimal cooperation between the various parts. Our Maker created us to bring forth a wonderful melody from our being, one that will bring joy not only to Him, but to ourselves and to others. Our Maker is also our Father. Because of the way He made us, we can experience and achieve much more by resting in Him than we could by following our own dreams or plans. But then we must acknowledge the way He put us together, and what role He assigned to each aspect of our being. *That* is your choice.

MEDITATE A MOMENT

1. Answer your body's question: Which situations put you in danger?
2. Answer the question your thoughts and emotions ask: With whom can I form relationships?
3. Answer your spirit's question: Who is my god?
4. Answer your heart's question: Who am I?
5. Do you normally make decisions based on what your body or emotions want (e.g. fear or what feels right)? Or are you indecisive and unsure?
6. What are you afraid of when you have to make a big decision? What are the 'What if?' questions that affect your choices?
7. Which relationships make you feel safe and respected, regardless? Why is this?
8. Which relationships leave you feeling inferior, confused, and inadequate? Why is this?
9. On a scale of 0 to 10, where 0 is 'non-existent' and 10 is 'extremely high', where does your self-respect lie? Why there?

Prayer

Thank you, Father, for creating me in such a fascinating way. I want to understand the different components of my make-up, and I want to respect each aspect's role and responsibility. I want to know and love myself with renewed passion. I also want to know, love, and serve You with all aspects of my being. I want to replace every half-baked conviction with your truth. Help me, Father, to understand these processes through your Holy Spirit, and to apply them until my whole life brings You praise. Please equip me to implement the necessary changes so that my inner harmony will grow to bring joy to You, to me and to others. I want to be part of the bigger plan You are bringing to fulfilment. I ask this in the Name of your Son, my Saviour, Jesus. Amen.

1. In *The Spiritual Brain* by Mario Beauregard, a Canadian neurobiologist, and Denyse O'Leary, a journalist.

2. *Strong's Exhaustive Concordance of the Bible*

3. By the International University for Advanced Study (SISSA) in Italy.

CHAPTER 9

COOPERATION

Effective inner management

Gear systems make movement possible. A gear transfers movement or power by engaging another gear or gears. Every gear needs to be in a specific position, exactly like the designer of the machine planned. Even the tiniest gear needs to give its full cooperation if the big machine or system is going to function correctly.

The right positioning of every part of the system is a prerequisite for functioning. This principle applies to humans as well. If you would like to make an effective, eternal impact on your environment, and know and serve you Creator with joy, you need inner order. You can only have it when every facet of your being is in the perfect position for it. For this you need knowledge about every aspect of the self, and insight into how it operates.

In the previous chapter, we broadly explained the various aspects of the self. A person is a soul who has a body, heart and spirit. Your emotions, thoughts, and will form part of the way you view life and how you interpret and connect with your physical and social environment. We touched on the role of the body in relation to the will to better understand Mariele's struggle. Now let's take a look at the role of emotions and thoughts.

Translating thought into action

If we want to express our will successfully, we need to arrange the different facets of our being in the correct order. If your will listens exclusively to your emotions or your body, you will waste precious energy. You will lurch through life in a daze, exhausted and frustrated. You will harm your self-image and your health, not to mention those around you.

Your will is enabled by three things: physical energy, a database in your head, and the convictions that motivate you. Without these, you cannot translate your thoughts into action. When your will does not 'get' your inner order, or rebel against it by listening to the demands of your body or your emotions, it will lead you astray. Your expectation will end in disappointment every time. Eventually, you will give up hope of ever changing. You will start to sceptically reject any suggestions of self-reform.

So, to whom is your will supposed to listen? We shall get to that, but for now you need to know that serving more than one master will tear your loyalty in two. The resulting inner conflict will play havoc with your effectiveness. Not only does your will need to remain loyal to one main authority, but it needs to give its full cooperation to the rest of the self, especially its two comrades, emotions and thoughts. Emotions play a very important role in your composition. Regardless of where they find themselves in the pecking order, they will greatly impact your inner management, your behaviour, and your effectiveness.

Why we have feelings

Among his many talents, my husband, Cobus, is an excellent *potjiekos* chef. His recipes are always colourful, flavoursome and tasty. When we have friends over, he cooks. His natural flair leads to dishes that will feel at home in any gourmet cookbook. A winning recipe should be perfectly flavoured with the right herbs and spices to give the best possible balance between taste and texture. Emotion plays much the same role in our lives. The 'taste' and 'texture' of our experiences depend on the emotions we go through when we have those experiences. Emotions make life colourful and flavoursome. Sometimes those flavours are sweet and exquisite, sometimes they're bitter and sour. Your emotions play a big part in the capturing of events. More about that later.

Emotions are contagious.

Emotions ought to enrich communication, but sometimes communication is pure emotion. Babies communicate mostly through their emotions. To ignore them when they cry would cause them trauma. When that happens, it is like one of those carnival mirrors – the image they have of themselves becomes totally skewed. They start to believe that they do not matter. This matter is discussed in greater detail in

Chapter 5. Hopefully such a child will later discover their true reflection in Jesus's eyes. His truth is the only objective measure of what we really look like. Loving, friendly, and sincere care reflect a child's true worth. Such positive social interaction even strengthens our immune system!

A lot of our social learning takes place through imitation. The neurons that are involved with this process, the so-called mirror neurons, are absolutely fascinating. They enable us to accurately mimic other people's behaviour.

Mirror neurons support learning and correct responses based on the intent they perceive. In other words, better understanding of someone's motives will lead to the right reaction.

Whether parents know this or not, children learn spontaneously by watching them go through the day. They are the child's primary role models. The child internalises their behaviour patterns simply by watching and learning. Thus, the parents' default response becomes the child's template for interpreting and reacting to events appropriately. Trauma, however, scrambles the input from other peoples' behaviour and causes children to respond in an inappropriate manner that can damage relationships.

Of all the animal types, humans have the most mirror neurons. Not only do they equip us to imitate behaviour, but they also enable us to learn new techniques and build relationships. These neurons enable us to perceive the emotions that other people project, making us part of their world. This is how we are able to show empathy and understanding.

Emotions are contagious. What you experience is consciously or subconsciously transmitted to others. Your social behaviour and ability to maintain relationships depend in large part on the efficiency of these neurons. The internationally acclaimed science journalist and author Daniel Goleman puts it this way: 'Our social interactions even play a role in reshaping our brain, through "neuroplasticity", which means that repeated experiences sculpt the shape, size, and number of neurons and their synaptic connections.'

That means that we are created to need love and kindness for our health and development. When your parents act in a kind, loving way, you spontaneously follow in their footsteps, paying respect to other people along the way. Unfortunately, the opposite also holds true. When somebody grows up in an environment that is devoid of love, they struggle to love and accept others.

Research bears out that we need to bond with other people emotionally, and that our very survival may depend on it. Your immune system requires solid, safe relationships. It has been proven that people recover quicker after an illness, surgery, or trauma when they are surrounded by people with whom they have good relationships. One also recovers more easily after a stressful event when safe, loving friendships support your hypothalamic pituitary adrenal (HPA) axis's return to its resting position (thus completing the fight-or-flight response). Oxytocin (the social hormone) is produced when loving and bonding with others. This hormone reduces the levels of cortisol, the stress hormone. Kind people around you lower your stress and support the restoration and the maintenance of your joy and peace. (See the previous chapter for more about this.)

Your emotions, therefore, enable you to form attachments to others in a healthy, empathetic way, and to be healthy and happy. They still need to be managed, however, before they can support you in such a way that you can play a useful role in society.

Emotional mismanagement

'Don't put the cart before the horse.' This old saying explains why we should not upset the right order. The horse has its place, as does the cart.

Inner order, where each aspect of our being is in its rightful place, depends on inner management. First and foremost, you have to deem each aspect of the self worthy of its role and function. That is a prerequisite for effective inner management. When you give your emotions free reign, they will take you on a wild roller coaster ride. That will confuse your focus (thoughts) to such an extent that it becomes hard to escape from certain repetitive thought patterns.

> **You can enjoy peace and joy as your default state of mind.**

When you have an intense experience, sensory data comes pouring in. Intense emotions usurp your attention and contribute to the capturing of the event. When you experience intense shock, it is usually accompanied by a whirlwind of emotions: fear, panic, confusion, astonishment, anger, and likely sorrow too – often all at once! Your emotions then tend to take over the decision-making process. That is exactly what paralysed Mariele. Her self-pity and despondency manipulated her will time and again.

Fear is a primary emotion. Its original purpose is to shield you from danger. When fear becomes a constant companion, your HPA axis (fight-or-flight cycle) can drain too much of your energy. This leads you to neglect what's left of you, and to suffer from emotional mismanagement. The goal after any negative experience is to restore rest (joy and peace). Your fight-or-flight response should run its course, so that your cortisol levels, heartbeat, blood pressure, and adrenalin levels may return to their normal resting position.

Constant or long-term fear will paralyse and inhibit you. Skewed perceptions and lies prevent the fear from being processed and handled properly. Following trauma, a person might form their own truth out of sheer desperation. You can also make blanket statements such as: 'Men only want one thing' (Mariele's conviction after her trauma). Your fear and your efforts to protect yourself from a repeat of the trauma keep these misperceptions alive and well.

Denial will also contribute to emotional mismanagement and the resulting damage to your whole self. You can't manage your emotions well if you can't or won't recognise them.

The earlier children can recognise and pinpoint emotions, the easier they will be able to manage them. This leads to increased emotional intelligence and gives these children an enormous advantage in life.

Emotional management means recognising and acknowledging your emotions and giving them their rightful place in your make-up. Mariele's fear that she would go through a similar trauma gave rise to certain limiting beliefs. Her heart was convinced that she would remain an easy target as long as she was beautiful. This 'truth' was propped up by her fear. Her fear and her limiting beliefs reinforced each other. These limiting assumptions settle in your mindset and play a huge role in determining your chosen behaviour. You should listen to your 'what ifs' and confront the thinking behind them. The moment Mariele recognised her fear as a mechanism to support her desire for protection, she realised the impact it had had on her whole being (including her weight). This prepared her to consider an alternative truth: *What would happen if I stopped being afraid of being beautiful?*

Recognising and describing your emotions bring some objectivity. It creates space to analyse the cause of your emotions and to choose appropriate, rational responses.

Anger, sadness, and frustration might sound like negative emotions, but they each play an important role in your maturing process, provided they (and other similar emotions) are managed correctly. Even frustration can become an effective tool in your healing process. More about that later.

Love and fear are diametrically opposed.

Positive emotions such as joy, cheerfulness, empathy, excitement, and enthusiasm fuel your immune system and other aspects of the self. Joy is about more than feeling happy. It has a strong connection to peace. These two are more a permanent state of mind than a fleeting emotion. Experiencing a joyous mindset is part of your inheritance as a child of God, yet few Christians have this disposition. This part of the book hopes to explain how you can enjoy peace and joy as your default state of mind.

Love and fear are diametrically opposed. Replacing fear-based behaviour is impossible without unconditional love. When you become aware of God's unconditional love for you and accept it (i.e. when you form a bond of love with Him), you turn away from the path of fear and start out on the road to re-creation. From fear to love. From lies to God's truth. Your way of thinking and reasoning has to adapt as well.

The riches of your thoughts

Whether you know it or not, you are analysing and reasoning all the time. Your behaviour displays your personal interpretation of matters to the world all the time. The psychologist Daniel Kahneman said: 'Cognition is embodied; you think with your body, not only with your brain.' Actually, you think with your whole being.

The body's memories of trauma sometimes manifest in therapy. A trauma victim might experience shortness of breath or heart palpitations when they recall certain events. Other people become nauseated, get headaches or become disoriented. The body also remembers.

Sure, the electro-chemical activity of your thoughts is limited to your brain, but every cell in your body is involved in processing and remembering. According to Kahneman's studies, the size of a person's pupils indicates the extent to which they are focusing. When you have to concentrate to make comparisons or take complex decisions, your pupils dilate, and your heart rate increases. As soon as you return to less taxing decisions or more mundane tasks, your pupils get smaller again. In daily living, there is non-negotiable cooperation between the visible and invisible aspects of the self.

Trying to figure things out purely on a physical level is not only time-consuming, but robs you of half your being. The data your senses import, is carefully filtered and processed. You naturally want to rationalise everything until it fits your personal framework of acceptability and confirms your assumptions. Every bit of sensory data reaches you through processed electro-chemical impulses. In a subsequent chapter, we will discuss in greater detail how the data gets processed further, until it influences your thoughts, will, emotions, spirit, and heart.

> **Our own expectations are often fertile
> soil for disappointment.**

Even though the brain is a fascinating organ, your conscious and subconscious thoughts (i.e. your mind) fall outside the relatively small area of the physical brain. Even though the body hosts the invisible parts of your being, your definition and impact stretch wider than your body and higher than your head. If you limit your being to your physical body, you will experience failure after failure, no matter how hard you try. Only when you recognise both aspects of your self, the visible and invisible, will your potential be able to develop fully.

Danny

It was September and everything was cool and green after a good rainy season in the Cape. The streets were full of people who had somewhere to be. Dwarfed by the trucks and 4x4 vehicles on the road, Danny was rushing to a church member's home in his small, blue Astra. While weaving his way through traffic, Danny was steaming. He was not in the mood for yet another crisis and the inevitable hysteria. Everybody expected him to be available at the drop of a hat. Every time he wasn't, there was hell to pay.

People would tell him that he had changed, that his heart had been hardened and that he failed to do the Lord's work. He was neglecting his flock, and God was disappointed, he would hear. If he did not toe the line, God would replace him, and he would not have any opportunities to serve. These 'warnings' did not emanate only from church members, but also from Marianne. She considered it her duty as the pastor's wife to keep Danny focused on his duties.

By the time Danny reaches Ashley's driveway, his heart is racing and the frown on his face looks as if it is etched there permanently. Ashley reaches him before he has switched off the car. It's been only 15 minutes since she called, but she did not expect anything less. Isn't that how it is supposed to work? Ashley's husband has turned violent again, traumatising her and the children. The children are crying and hide behind their mom while she introduces Danny to the police. This time she's had it. This really was the final straw.

Danny leads a big church. For over twelve years, he's been taking care of the flock. In the beginning he really liked it, but nowadays it gets increasingly difficult to see the upside.

He waited for a long time before making an appointment with me, but eventually he just could not continue. Not with the church and not with his marriage either. He just could not.

'It feels as if I've been emptied and now I'm slowly shrivelling,' Danny explains his reason for coming.

'Would you like to be filled to the brim again, Danny?' I ask.

He ponders the question for a while. I can almost hear his inner conversation. 'Yes, I would like to,' he answers eventually, 'but with the right stuff.'

A mixture of good and bad

Priorities change with the seasons. Every season has its demands. When you are a child, your responsibilities tend to be negligible and age-appropriate. Usually, they are reasonable and doable. As you grow older, these responsibilities grow with you, not to mention society's expectations. We expect ourselves and those around us to conform to certain stereotypical standards: 'Surely, by this time you ought to …' or 'Aren't you supposed to …?'

But sometimes you can't. Neither should you always be able to. Our own expectations and that of others are often fertile soil for disappointment. We run until we run out, give up, or break down – a shell of the person we once were.

When the soil of your heart receives good and bad seed, it produces inner strife and confusion. You struggle to discern effectively between acceptable and unacceptable, right and wrong. It is extremely exhausting and often yields fruit such as impatience, rebellion, bitterness, anger, and irritation. These fruits are not pleasant, especially for the people around you. They become the victims of your negative behaviour, while your self-reproach and guilt grow and grow. At some stage your body might decide to draw the line, as we have seen from a few stories so far.

The media sows to the soil of our hearts daily.

There are seeds of God's truth and seeds of deception. Unfortunately, both abound in marriages, prayer groups, and other church activities. They are equally prevalent outside the church, for example through motivational talks, mentors, leaders, and friends. The media sows to the soil of our hearts daily. We are exposed to the categorisation and stereotypes of society from a very early age.

Danny's church was not immune to the stereotype of what a pastor should be. He just had to conform, come what may. If he did not, it would mean that he was not a 'true' minister of the Word.

Danny's struggle was caused, in part, by the overwhelming amount of seeds that was sown into his life, often in nice, religious packaging. His heart regularly and readily received this seed in all humility from Marianne, her prayer group, and other church members. Over time, however, he started doubting what God wanted from him. The more 'instructions' he received, the more his confusion increased. He could not discern among the huge number of voices anymore. Was he simply too burnt out to do anything or was he, in fact, being disobedient? His inner conflict left him paralysed. He was bone-tired, confused, and angry. It was as if even the good seed did not want to sprout and grow anymore. Danny felt frustrated and ineffective.

The enabler

One of the main aspects of the self is your spirit. Your spirit is tied to the spiritual realm around you, whether you know it or not. Your spirit's biggest question is: 'Who is *my* God?'

Is that a simple question? It ought to be. However, I find it to be one of the most complex questions in life. The question is easy enough if you're a child of God who has to decide whether to worship God, Satan, or some idol. It becomes more complicated when you realise that your choices and behaviour simply do not 'connect' to your answer. Your behaviour – especially when no-one can see you or when you're under pressure – shows the true answer to your spirit's question.

Danny is a child of God. He chose to follow God. He has accepted Jesus, the Son of God, as his Saviour, and he has welcomed the Holy Spirit as his mentor and enabler.

In 1 Corinthians 6:17 Paul says: 'But the person who is joined to the Lord is one spirit with him' (NLT). God's Holy Spirit inhabits your heart and helps you to experience the impact of God's redemption work in your everyday life. He shows you who God truly is, so that you may know Him and create room for all the good He wants to impart to you.

He enables you to crucify the old person and He renews you inside out. He enables you to experience the full impact of the blood of Jesus, made available to you through his redemptive work. And as He equips you with knowledge and insight about who God is, and who you are in Him, you start turning the focus away from yourself and your own inability. You learn where your focus should go.

A golden key

A person's spirit can be influenced. We are easily awed by, or swept up in, the influences around us. Sometimes we do not even realise it, because we are ignorant. These influences can be confusing, especially if we do not understand what our spirits' role and responsibilities are. If we do not recognise that the spiritual realm is real or if we fail to understand how active it is, we can be deceived more easily. Sometimes, the spiritual realm can play a bigger part in our lives than the world we can see. As with any other aspect of our lives, we need knowledge to understand this world, as well as the role it plays in our lives, better.

The spiritual realm has its own hierarchies, rules, and laws. You can easily be drawn into its web of deception if you associate with certain people or events. Some associations become like a bridge that allows traffic to flow freely between the physical and the spiritual, unless you demolish the bridge or appoint gatekeepers to control access.

It is important to note the following:

- You – and every other person on earth – consist of body and spirit.
- Besides the visible world, there is an invisible spirit realm.
- Spiritual bonds with other people or spiritual entities enable you to influence them, but also to be influenced by them.
- Spiritual influences often represent a kingdom with its own set of rules and requirements.
- The rules and requirements (expectations) of such a kingdom can limit you or hold you in bondage. You can even become a slave of that kingdom.
- A slave mentality might become a lifestyle that keeps you from God's truth.
- Breaking free from such a spiritual stronghold might require a battle.
- Bondage to a spiritual kingdom will influence your thoughts.
- Deceived thinking hurts your choices, perceptions, and emotions.
- Your heart, and therefore your whole being, is influenced by your spiritual connections.

You pay a high price if you choose to remain unaware of, and ignorant about, this aspect of the self. You can't afford that. The only way your spirit can function safely and in harmony with the rest of you, is to be connected to the Holy Spirit, and to give Him permission to teach you, step by step, while you prayerfully guard your dependence on Him. He is by far the best sentry your inner world can have.

Danny takes action

Three weeks and a few sessions after Danny first came to see me, Marianne came along to my consulting room. I wanted to meet her. She had a rather large frame and an even larger presence.

Before I could settle in my chair, Marianne had already rearranged the coffee table books into neat piles and had turned the box of tissues towards the couch. The way it ought to be. 'There you are,' her posture seemed to say as she took Danny's hand firmly in hers. Her love for her husband and her dedication to him was plain to see in every gesture and facial expression. I immediately liked her. It was difficult not to. She radiated warmth and kindness.

Danny, however, sighed under his breath. His eyes remained shrouded when Marianne started to share her take on matters with me: 'Danny's biggest problem is that he doesn't listen anymore. Not to me, nor to God. Fortunately, we are here to help him now.'

She looked at her husband lovingly. He just stared straight ahead, not moving his hand in hers.

Danny and Marianne left, each with two questions they had to answer separately:

- Make a list of your roles in the marriage and the community.
- Make a list of your spouse's best/most attractive qualities (at least 25).

They were supposed to show their answers to each other at the next appointment, not before. During the following sessions, they discussed the lists. Quite a few misunderstandings and erroneous perceptions surfaced on both sides. We handled these together. Danny's biggest breakthrough came when he was able to throw off the burden of false responsibilities. What God expects of you and what society expects of you, are often very different animals. To maintain this distinction, the brave pastor had to implement a host of changes. It was not easy. Managing expectations must surely be one of the key elements in a relationship.

Marianne, on the other hand, had to learn where Marianne began and where Marianne ended. Her tendency to simply take over and marshal matters meant that she often trespassed on Danny's territory while neglecting her own. She sincerely thought she was helping – and doing a better job. However, she had to retreat from Danny's territory and rediscover her own. Danny also had to reclaim his boundaries and take control of his relationships, choices, behaviour, and calling.

> **To be fully you, you have to stay alive (the body's task), benefit from relationships with others by employing your thoughts and emotions (the task of your heart), and live in unity with God (the task of your spirit).**

Danny's re-creation story gives one hope. His willingness to listen to anyone and everyone's 'advice' and 'warnings' (and believing them) led to an inability to hear what the Holy Spirit was trying to say to him through God's Word. He focused on his wife and church too much, and worried more about keeping them happy than pleasing his Heavenly Father. The connections between him and all the people in his life left him vulnerable to input and suggestions that were not always helpful or appropriate, even if they were accompanied by the best intentions. He had to realise that he needed a heart-connection with God more than he needed head-connections with people. Shifting his focus back to his first love, his Heavenly Father, became the springboard for his recovery. His spirit had to be fused to the Holy Spirit once more.

Danny's influence as a preacher grew exponentially as his re-creation journey progressed, because his fear of (reverence for) God became bigger than his fear of people (including Marianne). His emptiness soon disappeared as he filled his being with treasures that moth and rust could not destroy. Out of this place of abundance, Danny trained to become emotionally fit. He managed his emotions in a way that prevented them from taking over when church members demanded his time and attention. Every anxiety and sorrow, every reason for excitement or frustration could be managed to work for him in the light of God's truth. His inner conflict, confusion, and overactive guilt were channelled to peace. Danny's life was called to order, and he could return to his calling, only this time he was cooperating with God's Spirit.

Marianne was right after all. It *was* Danny's hearing that had to change. Wasn't that what she said?

Conclusion

The different elements of your being (body, spirit and heart) each have their own characteristics that allow them to execute their responsibilities with ease. When the various elements of your being communicate and cooperate, you are mobilised to be a fully functional human.

To be fully you, you have to stay alive (the body's task), benefit from relationships with others by employing your thoughts and emotions (the task of your heart), and live in unity with God (the task of your spirit). From this position of harmony, you can grow as a person and become bigger than your own narrow interests. Your life's course can benefit you, other people, and the kingdom you belong to.

When the different aspects do not execute their respective tasks or end up in the wrong order, it becomes very difficult to maintain inner harmony. Someone needs to supervise the self and hold the various aspects accountable for executing their responsibilities. In the next chapter we shall look at this crucial step.

MEDITATE A MOMENT

1. What is your natural resting position after a negative experience?
2. What does your inner sanctuary look like – the place you go to after such an event?
3. Sometimes your recovery spot is not a place of joy. If this is true for you, are you willing to break it down? Will you start building a place of joy in its stead?
4. What percentage of your day is filled with joy?
5. If less than 75% of your day is filled with joy: What are the other emotions / moods you experience during the day? Why?
6. In the normal course of events, are you able to recognise, name and describe your emotions?
7. Think about your emotional vocabulary. Is it rich and varied or somewhat anaemic? How many words can you call on to describe your emotions?
8. Think about the voices you usually listen to. Do you mostly listen to other people's needs and expectations like Danny? Do you mostly listen to your body's demands for immediate gratification? Do you mostly listen to your emotions because you just want to feel better?
9. How would your spirit answer the question 'Who is *your* God?'?
10. Name the behaviour and choices that contradict your answer to the previous question. Why?

Prayer

King of my life, thank you for making me so wonderfully.
You wove me together with attention to every fine detail and
made each aspect of me a specialist in its own right.
I understand that each aspect has its own specific responsibilities,
and that I should not disturb its position and role out of ignorance.
I surrender to You and ask that You would renew my thoughts so that
I can function in unity with your truth. I want to cultivate thought
patterns that reflect your victory. Marvellous Creator God,
thank you for the privilege of choice.
Thank you for a will that is free to act on my thoughts and decisions.
Lord, it is a wonderful gift, but also an enormous responsibility. Teach
me how to prevent my will from becoming confused, exhausted, or just
plain lazy. Let it never abdicate its role. Teach me to use my will to
execute sound decisions that are good for me. Today I choose to
obey You in my thoughts and the execution of my will.
Creator God, thank you for the contribution of emotions. It brightens
up my life and brings flavour and colour to life's ordinary experiences.
I want to be emotionally fit and return to my sanctuary,
my place of joy, again and again.
I would love to establish my own place of joy, Father. Help me
to grow my capacity for joy and to have a zest for life.
You allow me to. Thank you for granting me this gift. I want my default
emotion to be joy, not worry and anxiety. Thank you, my King, that
I may surrender my spirit to you now. Purify me from any spiritual
debris and any spiritual bonds that are not from You. Free me so that
nothing will limit me or keep me away from your truth.
I want your Holy Spirit to feel at home inside me. I invite You, o Holy
Spirit, to teach me more about You. I want to experience You as the
sovereign Councillor and Enabler in my life, down to its smallest aspect.
Thank you for this possibility. Thank you for the perfect work
of my Saviour, Jesus, on the cross that makes it possible to
have the Holy Spirit as my Companion.
Please prepare me now for the work that still lies ahead to establish
your order in me. I want to live effectively in your Kingdom by
the power I get from being one with You.
In the Name of your Son, Jesus, my Saviour.
Amen.

PART 3

HOW WE CHANGE

Practical steps on the road
to truth and wholeness

ongratulations on making it this far! In Part 1 you saw a few of the ways in which our lives can be derailed. You also saw how our best efforts to fix things often make matters worse, leaving us discouraged and despondent. On the positive side, you learned that you are not alone and that people in similar situations to yours have managed to get their lives back on track.

> Your life will be aligned to the ultimate Truth,
> bringing you peace, joy, and wisdom.

You have started your own recovery by finding out in Part 2 how God knitted you together. Long-term change is hard, if not impossible, without this knowledge. Acquiring self-knowledge remains a life-long journey, and you only ever make progress when you consult your Maker. He is the only one who can shed light on where you come from, the reason why you are here, and the way you are put together.

Now that you have built a solid foundation, you are ready to take on Part 3 – How we change. It contains practical steps and pointers that you can follow on the road to wholeness. These chapters should be tackled chronologically, in an attentive and prayerful manner.

In Chapter 10 you will see how to move from chaos to order, starting with your inmost being and moving out in ever widening circles. You will learn to orient yourself to the truth found in God's Word until it permeates every part of your being and makes you more resilient than ever. In Chapter 11 you will learn how this new orientation changes the way you perceive and act on information that enters your world. You will become acquainted with four steps to effect change and learn to implement them successfully. However, success needs to be maintained. That is the focus of Chapter 12, where you will also learn the importance of forgiveness and a solid sense of identity to stay on track.

How can you align your life to the ultimate Truth? How can you experience peace, joy, and wisdom in ever greater measure? The principles and steps that will lead you there are found in the following pages.

CHAPTER 10

HARMONY

When hierarchy leads
to harmony

Chaos brings a need for order. Order that stems from fear is like being ruled with an iron fist. It often leads to rebellion, which demolishes any trace of order anyway. Order that originates in love brings life. In turn, life brings energy, and energy creates order from chaos.

Order requires that each component of the bigger whole must be in its designated position. Arranging your inner world means assigning a dedicated space to each component. Order determines what the main thing should be, and how the rest should slot in.

> **A malfunction in our collective being threatens our earthly existence and impacts eternity.**

It happens on a micro as well as a macro level. Our solar system reflects order on a macro level. Each planet's position relative to the sun has been carefully calibrated and speaks of a brilliant Creator. The earth is in exactly the right spot to make life on the planet possible.

Order can also be observed on a micro level. Each atom contains protons and neutrons and electrons that move around the nucleus in extremely intricate energy circuits. Each of these subatomic particles has a particular function that helps the relevant element do what it was created for. If the components deviate from their correct position, the environment will degrade to complete chaos, on a micro as well as a macro level.

The human race's very survival depends on the role and function of the sun in the solar system, as well as the atoms in each element, to maintain their carefully plotted positions. The location of the tiniest particle impacts the greater environment. As far as our lives are concerned, we depend on the position, role, and function of each aspect of our collective being. A malfunction here does not just threaten our earthly existence; it impacts eternity.

Inner order precedes outer order

In Part 1 we looked at the second law of thermodynamics, which says that, in any system, there is a gradual decline of energy. When energy is converted from one form to another, some of it is lost in the process forever. The amount of usable energy declines. Order degenerates into disorder.

If you do not pay attention to your inner life, it will tend to become chaotic. It takes energy and willpower to sustain order. Unfortunately, we do not always have willpower and, as we have learnt from Mariele's story, trauma will confuse you to such an extent that your heart will surrender its position and role, leaving you exhausted and on the brink of giving up.

The heart is central to your being.

Inner order that flows from every aspect of your self, but especially your heart when it is in the correct position, can help to bring about outward order. When that manifests, your presence and behaviour will naturally promote order in your environment, often subconsciously.

But what does that look like in practice? What comes first, and what follows? Where is your heart supposed to be? A study of God's Word shows us the direction we must take to embark on a journey of restoration. This journey will help to re-create your inner life and bring you in line with God's truth.

First-hand experience leads to conviction

A study of the almost 1 000 references to the word 'heart' in *Strong's Exhaustive Concordance of the Bible* (*leb* in Hebrew and *kardia* in Greek) sheds a lot of light on the real position of the heart in our lives. My mom wrote every single one down in her elegant hand. I treasure this document and often derive great joy from it. A handful of references will prove the point.

In 1 Peter 3:4 the apostle refers to 'the hidden person of the heart'. He is referring to a person's core identity. It is hidden, but not forgotten. The heart is central to your being. 'Who am I?' is the heart's biggest question.

You ought to compare your experiences with God's truth.

In Exodus 3:14 the Creator God introduces Himself as 'I AM WHO I AM'. God is perfect, perfectly whole, and complete in Himself. But who are we, the ordinary created people? How is our self-definition formed?

People learn every day. We expand our knowledge by reading and listening. Often, this knowledge stems from someone else's experience, so it is second-hand or indirect. However, the knowledge we gain from direct, intense experience penetrates deeply into our being. It has the power to rewrite our inner story – that is why we talk about writing on the tablets of our hearts. This type of knowledge changes our opinions, assumptions, and consequently, also our behaviour and choices. (More about this in the following chapter.)

Change as a result of personal experiences is often seen at the neural level. Research has shown how traumatic experiences can change a person's DNA, and consequently that of their offspring. The stress hormone, cortisol, plays no small part in this. Physical aspects of DNA strings can be influenced by human intention.[1] (Epigenesis, the study of how experiences change the functioning of your genes, is discussed in several chapters.)

Experiences have great potential to bring about change. However, such change does not necessarily line up with God's truth. When you experience something, you ought to compare it with God's truth as He reveals it in his Word.

God's truth must be the most important first-hand experience of our lives. *This truth circumcises your heart and rewrites the answer to the question 'Who am I?' You belong to Him, and you are his beloved.* When your heart finds rest in this knowledge, your re-creation process can start. In Deuteronomy 30:6 (NIV) we read:

The LORD your God will circumcise your hearts and the hearts of your descendants, so that you may love him with all your heart and with all your soul, and live.

If you can, read Deuteronomy 10:16 and Romans 2:29 as well.

So, you can rest in Him, knowing that He is more committed to your healing than you could ever be. When He circumcises your heart, neither your 'previous life' nor your genetic inheritance can determine your identity. Instead, *his* words, *his* truth, and your experiences with *Him* becomes your heart's message.

A multitude of facets

We serve a God who richly endowed his Word with symbolism and multiple layers of meaning. The physical character of your heart and the rest of your body illustrate a great deal (but by no means all) of your invisible qualities. Let's take a look at the various ways in which our physical attributes act as metaphors for the psychological aspects of our being.

The focus of our investigation in this chapter falls on the heart. This organ weighs a mere 300 gram, yet it pumps approximately 7 000 litres of blood through the body every day! It filters and purifies. The heart pumps life in the form of oxygenated blood to the rest of the body and carries oxygen-poor blood to the lungs to be topped up with oxygen once more. This process is crucial to keep the body going. Likewise, your invisible heart has a duty to filter and to purify. It is constantly working to filter and remove the impurities of lies and deception, rejection, and ambushes. It needs to discern and to judge.

In Biblical times the high priest had to lead and exhort God's people, the Israelites, with truth and insight. His breastplate that signifies his responsibilities was worn on his chest, close to the heart:

> 'So Aaron shall bear the names of the sons of Israel on the breastplate of judgment over his heart, when he goes into the holy place, as a memorial before the LORD continually. And you shall put in the breastplate of judgment the Urim and the Thummim, and they shall be over Aaron's heart when he goes in before the LORD. So, Aaron shall bear the judgment of the children of Israel over his heart before the LORD continually.'
>
> – EXODUS 28:29–30

In Ecclesiastes 8:5 we also read: '… a wise man's heart discerns both time and judgment.' Your heart should be able to discern divine seasons and to judge righteously with insight. Such a person makes an effective impact in society.

John and Beatrice Lacey indicated in 1970 already that the brain sends commands to the heart via a specialised nervous system.[2] The heart duly reacts by either considering the message or by expediting it if a stressful situation has been communicated. The volume of blood that it pumps can increase from its resting volume of 5 litres per minute to as much as 25 litres per minute. The Laceys also proved that the heart sends messages to the brain. The brain not only receives these messages, but obeys them. A few neurocardiologists in New York found that the heart has its own nervous system with close to 40 000 neurons. That is more or less the same number of neurons we find in the subcortical parts of the brain. These neurons allow the heart to consider and judge instructions and information, and to sometimes take decisions independently from the brain.

The Laceys' research field was psychophysiology, but other fields soon joined: neurophysiology, cardiology, and neuroanatomy. A new discipline, neurocardiology, was formed.

So far, research in the field of neurocardiology has found that the heart has a complex neural network. It is called the intrinsic cardiac nervous system (ICNS), or 'heart-brain' for short. It consists of combinations of the neurons, ganglia, neurotransmitters, proteins, and support cells.

The heart-brain enables the heart to function independently from the cranial brain and often the autonomic nervous system (ANS) too. It learns, forms memories, makes decisions, and even feels and senses!

It is all due to the specialised neural circuitry between the heart and the brain (and the rest of the body).

The heart communicates through four pathways:
1. Biophysical (pulse wave)
2. Biochemical (neurotransmitters and hormones)
3. Neurological (nervous system)
4. Energetic (electromagnetic fields)

Messages from the heart to the brain are called afferent (inward) signals; messages from the brain to the heart are called efferent (outward) signals. These pathways operate mainly via the vagal nerves, a nervous system that consists of a multi-branch network that links the brain with the body. The majority of fibres in the vagal nerve are afferent, so it seems as if more information is sent to the brain (from the heart) than the other way around.

Afferent inputs often affect the brain's electrical activity. It can either inhibit or enhance brain activity. How the heart communicates with the brain depends on the heart's rhythms. More about that later.

Brain activity, especially in the thalamic part, is modulated through the pattern and stability of the heart rhythm's afferent inputs. (Neural bursts do not necessarily have that effect on brain activity.) These inputs can influence attention and focus, motivation, and even emotional processing – all aspects that are vital to effective functioning.

The heart also seems to act as a hormonal gland that produces certain hormones, such as:

- Atrial Natriuretic Factor (ANF), also called the balance hormone, assists with the regulation of adrenal glands, kidneys, and various centres in the brain.
- Oxytocin, also called the social hormone, is both a hormone and a neurotransmitter. This powerful hormone plays an important role in bonding, empathy, and healing (as mentioned before).

The heart and trauma

Your physical heart shows further correlation with your unseen heart in the way it responds to and is affected by stressful or traumatic events. Negative events often seem to precipitate heart failure, just as positive events seem to strengthen heart health.

Stress triggers emotions such as anxiety, worry, concern, frustration, fear, despair and hopelessness, annoyance, and irritation. This causes secondary psychological processes that directly impact various physiological systems.

> **Resilience is the capacity to prepare for, recover from, and adapt in the face of stress, adversity, trauma, or challenge.**

Trauma can be dealt with by 'splitting' (also referred to as 'gating'), i.e. separating the facts of the trauma event from their emotional burden. This affords the victim time to process and emotionally 'digest' the experience.

If you want to face or confront a traumatic memory in the most effective manner as part of your restoration process, it often requires you to recall both the facts and the emotions connected to that event.

Emotions, more than thoughts, activate physiological changes (especially stress responses) and support a few vital role-players in energy regulation. In other words, where would you like to spend your energy? What deserves your precious energy?

During the Covid-19 pandemic, humanity was challenged in many ways. An enormous amount of emotional (as well as physical and mental) energy is required to deal with the various setbacks, shocks, limitations, and losses in many areas of our lives. Many people showed, and still show, a remarkable ability to 'bounce back' and even grow from this global disaster. People refer to this ability as human resilience. Resilience is the capacity to prepare for, recover from, and adapt in the face of stress, adversity, trauma, or challenge. You need strong resilience and proper emotional management to function effectively with healthy self-regulation.

Circumstances   Victor

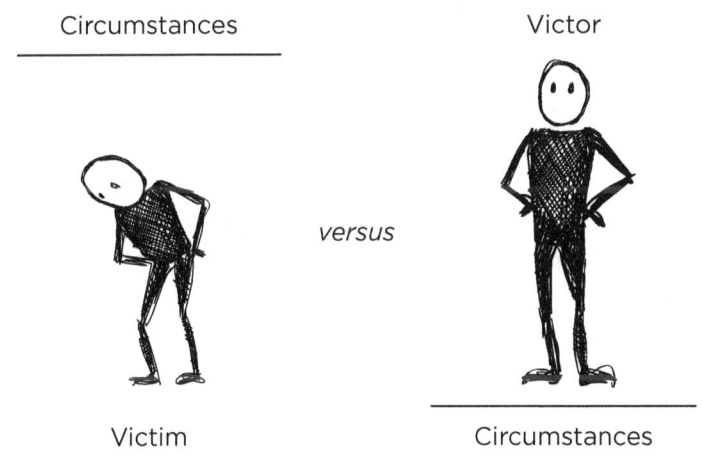

versus

Victim   Circumstances

A victor typically has resilience in spades, as well as effective emotional regulation, and a healthy sense of coherence. A victor views life as meaningful and lives with a conscious purpose, managing the various demands and enjoying the basic blessings of life.

There are three areas of resilience:
1. Physical resilience finds expression in strength, health, responsible discipline, respect, encouragement, and care.
2. Emotional resilience leads us to attach the proper emotional 'weight' or value to specific experiences so that we can choose a fitting response. Effective metabolising ('digestion') of overwhelming emotional experiences, especially trauma-related ones, which leads to emotional insight and fitness.

Any experience has the potential to make people more adaptable and emotionally flexible, to grow their emotional vocabulary, to improve the way they verbalise, and to strengthen their powers of association. To realign experiences to God's truth delivers fruit of wisdom.

3. Spiritual resilience is evidenced by strong, stable intuition of the spirit world and finely tuned discernment.

   Such a person is dependable and displays insight into the Source of Life, our Creator God, through his Spirit.

   Knowing God and getting to know Him is this person's highest priority. Out of that flows faith, commitment, wisdom, and being receptive to new revelation to grow from. The whole process of change – true transformation – depends on this kind of knowledge. We will discuss it in detail in the following chapter.

The emotional heart

Your heart feels. Joy is a state of the heart. So is fear. Rejection or severe loss can even change the physical shape of the heart (see 'Broken heart syndrome' on p. 148). As we said previously, emotions add value to an experience. Emotions also contribute to physical and mental health. Positive emotions increase health, as does intentional focus on things that are true, noble, just, pure, lovely, and of good report (Phil 4).

Developing an attitude of gratitude strengthens health and stable emotional management. We shall discuss gratitude in more detail in the last chapter. Gratitude includes appreciation, which seems to improve brain regulation systems and autonomic nervous system (ANS) functioning. Stronger immune and cognitive functioning is picked up by human/machine interfaces when gratitude is exercised habitually.

The heart's afferent signals to the brain's various cognitive structures also impact emotions significantly.

Heart rate variation (HRV) measures the beat-to-beat changes that normally occurs. HRV reflects information's emotional 'weight'. A high HRV indicates healthy functioning and resilience in all three areas. A low HRV indicates emotional depletion, possible chronic stress, illness, or inadequate functioning on various levels.

Research has shown that prayers of gratitude and honest, heartfelt love result in higher HRV and therefore higher functioning. Heart rate variation is a well-researched indicator of your capacity to regulate your emotional and behavioural responses.

The matter of coherence

Effective alignment and the harmony it brings between the various aspects of self (body, spirit and heart with your emotions, will, and mind) seem to support improved focus and concentration, healthy and positive social connections, and appropriate emotional management. It improves your creative and intuitive ability, as well as your ability to listen and focus in order to have rational interpretation and engagement. Effective collaboration or coherence will also enhance your response to stressors (triggers) and challenges in general.

Coherence describes the joining of various parts in a meaningful way for stronger efficiency. It can be seen in clarity of thought, speech, and emotional composure. Coherence brings correlation, connectedness, and efficient utilisation of your energy resources.

If one individual achieves coherence, it impacts the people around him. True transformation happens when coherence multiplies from one individual to the broader community (family, friends, and co-workers). Change requires changing your expectations, changing your 'normal', and regularly challenging the familiar. (More about this in the next chapters.) Change on a micro level will eventually impact the bigger environment. Transformation equals wholeness and global order, where the whole is greater than the sum of its parts.

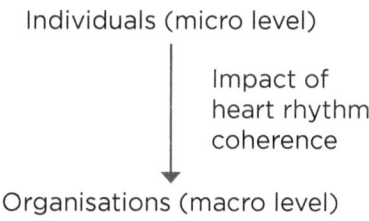

Individuals (micro level)

Impact of heart rhythm coherence

Organisations (macro level)

In a coherent company, individual members have the freedom to be true to their individuality while still nourishing cohesion within the team's vision.

The energetic heart

Your heart also communicates through a magnetic field that is 100 times stronger than that of your brain. This magnetic field maintains a perimeter around the body of almost one metre. Human and animal hearts display natural inner magnetic responses.

A person's emotional state is encoded in the heart's magnetic field, which communicates it throughout the body and into the external environment. Your emotions quite literally change the atmosphere!

When two individuals start to talk and their conversation deepens, a beautiful interconnectedness becomes measurable in the electromagnetic fields around them. Through these fields, signals are transmitted and detected by the participating parties. After only four minutes, there is a measurable synchronisation in some of their physiological responses. It is your nervous system that picks up, and responds to, the other person's magnetic field.

There seems to be a significant degree of EEG-to-ECG (brain-to-heart) signal transfer through the skin, but in non-physical contact the signals are transferred from the sender's heart (ECG) to the recipient's brain (EEG).

Sender   Receiver

The degree of coherence in the receiver's heart rhythms appears to determine whether his brain waves synchronise to the other person's heart.

Researchers have found that recipients exhibit greater sensitivity in registering the encoded electromagnetic signals and information patterns radiated by others when they are in a physiologically coherent state themselves.

The good news is that you seem to be less vulnerable to negative influences from others if you are coherently stable. Therefore, a joyful individual might be able to influence someone battling with a less positive mood. We will discuss the dynamics of influence in more detail in the coming chapters.

Dr Lew Childre Jr, founder of the HeartMath Institute, stated: 'Since emotional processes can work faster than the mind, it takes a power stronger than the mind to bend perception, override emotional circuitry and provide us with intuitive feeling instead. It takes the power of the heart.' Your heart matters!

Remember, as you expand your understanding of the physical heart, you will also grasp the profound responsibilities of the unseen heart and how they manifest. However, it is very important not to compare every function of the physical body with unseen aspects of the self. As explained previously, the physical body is ranked lowest of the aspects that make up the self, while the non-physical heart and the spirit are ranked higher.

Let's take a look at more correlations between the physical (visible) and the spiritual (invisible) aspects of self involved in long-term change.

The hearing and seeing heart

In the same way that people have visible and invisible hearts, they have visible (physical) and invisible (spiritual) senses.

Your senses are gateways. Each one plays a crucial role in the interpretation of your environment and cooperation with other people. They feed our inner selves with data and leaves the processing to the rest of the self. Data from our physical senses can be clearly observed in different parts of the brain.

However, there are invisible senses that work within the very depths of our being. We ignore these invisible senses at our peril. The heart, which forms part of the psyche, can hear, see, and feel.

Our invisible senses are far more powerful than the visible ones – in rank, sensitivity, and impact. This will become clear in the chapter about their role in the process to change.

The heart experiences a variety of positive and negative emotions such as joy and excitement, but also sadness, regret, and anxiety.

Despair, disillusionment, shock, and betrayal can lead to a wounded, sick, or broken heart:

- In Psalm 109:22, the psalmist says that his heart is 'wounded' within him.
- In Proverbs 13:12, we read: 'Hope deferred makes the heart sick.'
- According to Psalm 69:20–21, the heart can also be broken by shame and dishonour.
- Only the Creator of our hearts knows how to heal a broken heart.
- According to Isaiah 61:1, God sends his Servant 'to heal the broken-hearted'. In Luke 4:21, Jesus said that He was the Servant who had come to do the mending.

The Hebrew word for 'heart' that is used here ('leb' and 'shabar') indicate a broken or fragmented heart. A wounded or a broken heart is desperate to find help. When your heart is in that state, you should be very careful about whom you trust. Fortunately, God assures us in his Word: 'The sacrifices of God are a broken spirit, A broken and a contrite heart – These, O God, You will not despise' (Ps 51:17).

> **It is the heart's posture that enables us to truly see and hear.**

The cardiologist Dr Sondeep Jauhar made the following profound statement: 'A record of our emotional life is written on our hearts.' He explains how trauma and emotional turmoil can change the very shape of our hearts. Broken heart syndrome reveals how the heart can change to a similar shape than the Japanese takotsubo vase. Stressful events such as loss of a loved one or big disappointments will not only affect your metaphorical heart, but can cause physical change, manifesting your emotional pain in takotsubo cardiomyopathy.

I am grateful for the many Biblical references to joyful or rejoicing hearts. It is good and beneficial for us to have such hearts. 'A merry heart does good, like medicine,' says Proverbs 17:22.

The heart needs its invisible senses to aid discernment and decision-making. You can have eyes, but remain blind. You can have ears, but remain deaf. You can perceive things, but never experience truth. When you are blinded by deception, hard of hearing due to calloused ears or embittered by hurt, you tend to isolate. This hinders you from grasping God's truth. Paul admonishes the Ephesians: 'You should no longer walk as the rest of the Gentiles walk, in the futility of their mind, having their understanding darkened, being alienated from the life of

God, because of the ignorance that is in them, because of the blindness of their heart' (Eph 4:17–18).

Jesus tells his disciples: 'Blessed are your eyes for they see, and your ears for they hear' (Matt 13:16), but He also speaks about people whose ears are hard of hearing and who have closed their eyes. They do not want to see or hear, lest they understand with their hearts and turn to God for healing.

So, the question is: *Do you want to hear God's truth and understand it with your heart?*

The heart's observation plays an important part in effective functioning. A massive responsibility hinges on the way you view the world. How you see it forms the first step in the re-creation process. The next chapter will explain this in more detail.

The condition of your heart is the biggest factor that determines the quality of your observation. Throughout the Bible, we read about people who see without perceiving, and who hear without understanding. Clearly, the required kind of seeing and hearing has little to do with your physical senses. It is the heart's posture that enables us to truly see and hear. *The heart's invisible senses are among the true factors that drive change.*

Your story journal

If you give a child a pencil and a piece of paper, you're bound to have a drawing in no time. Likewise, if you give the heart an experience, it will paint pictures about it on the walls of your inner life. And, as we have learnt earlier, the pictures and stories that are written on your heart impact your whole being. This is why the writer of Proverbs says:

> Let not mercy and truth forsake you; Bind them around your neck, Write them on the tablet of your heart.
>
> – Proverbs 3:3

Paul also underscores the importance of the things we write on the tablets of our hearts:

> You are our epistle written in our hearts, known and read by all men; clearly you are an epistle of Christ, ministered by us, written not with ink but by the Spirit of the living God, not on tablets of stone but on tablets of flesh, *that is*, of the heart.
>
> – 2 Corinthians 3:2–3

As data flows into your body, it is categorised and filed so that it can be available if you need to recall it later. Sensory data and how you interpret it form your experiences. We might also illustrate it as follows:

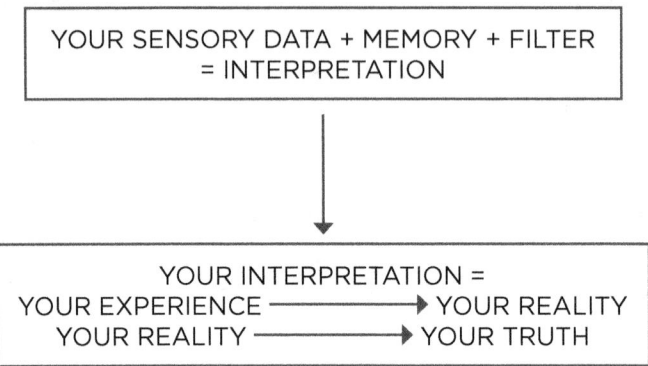

Your truth is recorded on your heart, clear and permanent as tattoos. The decisions we make at heart level are mostly influenced by this recorded information. Whatever is engraved on your heart talks loudest when you have to make a decision. These choices manage the rest of your psyche and become visible through your body.

Derrick

The late afternoon sunbathed the boardroom's windows in hues of yellow, orange, and apricot. Everybody in the cavernous room knew that normal work hours had long since passed, but nobody made a move to leave. In the dark director's chair was Derrick. He was slumped forward with his head in his hands and his elbows on the big walnut table. It was clear that he had not had proper sleep in days. He was overtired and highly irritable, yet he tried to hide his anxiety from the others.

His company was in big trouble, and days of meetings and negotiations had not delivered anything in the way of a viable solution. The crisis had been a long time coming, and he was angry with himself for not listening to advice much earlier.

Every now and again the word 'Why?' reverberated through

his thoughts. He struggled to discern between guilt, fear, and worry. The rest of the board looked equally desperate and on edge. Derrick looked up slowly. The atmosphere in the room was loaded with conflict and resentment. Nobody was in the mood to listen to anyone anymore.

Derrick's gaze travelled from one director to the next. The recent problems had dragged on too long. The toll it had exacted on everybody was plain to see. Actually, they had lost confidence in him a long time ago, and he could understand why.

When Derrick walked into my study, his military posture and body language left no doubt as to who would be in charge. His body sat down on the couch, but his attitude invaded the entire room. He is a tall man, and his legs reached all the way underneath the coffee table. His loose-fitting clothes indicated that he had recently lost a few kilograms.

'Well,' he said, obviously irritated. 'Apparently I have to be here.' His hands were fiddling with his phone the whole time.

'Why?' I asked.

'Beats me. Our company's consultant insisted. I do not know how it's supposed to help.'

'For how long have you been this frustrated, Derrick?' I asked. Seasons of suffering were etched deep into his face. I really wanted to hear his answer.

My client looked confused for a moment, yet he searched himself for an answer. 'I suppose since my company's troubles started. I never imagined my dream would turn into such a nightmare. I'm between a rock and a hard place, and I do not know where to turn.'

> **Some people deny reality and think
> that they have moved on.**

Derrick looked into the distance. I sat quietly and gave him time to consider the rest of his answer. A while later he said in a hoarse voice: 'Come to think of it, it started when Lydia cheated on me. Or rather, when I found out about it.' He looked up. 'It's been a hell of a road since then, I can tell you,' he said, visibly tired.

Derrick's story was indeed a sad one. After seventeen years of being happily married, as far as he was concerned anyway, his wife's infidelity caught him completely off-guard. His heart shattered in a million pieces under the weight of disillusionment.

But surely, he should have moved on by now, not so? 'Moving on' is a relative term. Every person interprets it in their own way and has their own expectations around it. To truly and effectively move on, various things have to happen. Some people deny reality and think that they have moved on. Some people harden their hearts toward the guilty party in order to protect themselves from future hurt and think that they have moved on. Does this ring any bells? But truly moving on in a way that reflects eternal values involves confrontation, embracing the pain and injustice and discomfort, but also the potential to see something worthwhile growing out of it in due course.

Derrick's pain blinded him to any good and beautiful things.

'I'm not the Derrick I used to be. I don't know myself anymore. I used to be able to handle a ton of pressure. Nowadays I feel like an animal in a cage. A damn small cage.'

Our conversation continued, exploring how Derrick ended up in the cage in the first place, and what the small cage represented. Derrick had to give his own interpretation of the main events in his life. He was full of inner turmoil, and every so often his angered threatened to erupt.

Often, signs of anger indicate the presence of fear.

'What is your biggest "what if" at the moment, Derrick?' I asked.

He leaned back, crossed his legs and gazed at the ceiling. He gave my question fair consideration.

'What if I … lose *everything*?' he asked. He looked straight at me. I could see the fear in his eyes. His house of cards was starting to tumble. His reputation in the business world was in tatters and his marriage was over.

'What would it mean for you to lose everything?' I insisted.

Derrick answered, his whole demeanour of earlier now stripped of its bravado. 'Who would I, Derrick, be if that happened?'

Trauma hijacks your inner order

The company that employed Derrick as managing director was sinking. For months, Derrick thought his management team's performance was to blame – and he was right to an extent – but the actual reason for the crisis stemmed from his marital trauma. Lydia, Derrick's wife, had broken his heart long before the company started taking on water. Her affair with his business partner completely blindsided him. The double betrayal crippled his leadership and hindered him from effectively steering the company. However, the disarray inside him and the chaos in his company had to reach crisis levels before he became desperate enough to seek help – a hard thing to do for some people.

Initially, Derrick's company was quick and successful. People banked on their services and the company built up a solid reputation. From the cleaner to the directors, everyone understood their role and executed it to the best of their ability. Until that fateful day when Derrick simply got up and walked out in the middle of a planning meeting. A constant reminder of everything that was robbed from him, work just became too much to bear. He wanted to escape the terrible pain and rejection that was foisted on him by the two failed relationships. His interest in his company plummeted so fast that each director had to accept and designate new responsibilities on the fly.

Nobody could understand why he acted so strangely.

> **Our Maker sees and picks up every
> fragment of our shattered hearts
> and makes something spectacular
> out of it.**

Over time Derrick became more inaccessible to his directors. He was either at the golf course (rather than his office) or snapping at his colleagues for 'wasting' his time and 'majoring on minors'. He laid down his leadership role, necessitating the other directors to step in and take decisions outside their areas of expertise. The company and its employees suffered. Months of mismanagement translated into bad feedback from clients, negative conversations around the water-cooler, and serious dents in the bottom line. The managing director's personal life was also showing clear signs of mismanagement.

At last, with the possibility of bankruptcy looming ever larger, the directors found out about his personal crisis and urged Derrick to follow the consultant's advice to seek help.

The knock-on effect of Derrick's broken heart circled ever wider. Fortunately, the healing of such a heart can also have far-reaching impact. For Derrick and his company, the healing potential may have been bigger than the original damage.

Treasure from trash

If Jesus had to live among us in human form today, what would his impact be?

A few years ago, there was a movie that illustrated this possibility. A vulnerable, middle-aged woman dared to declare her love to a man after knowing him for a considerable time. Without her knowing it, the man in question was Jesus, who was staying in the town temporarily. He tenderly and respectfully told her that he was not the love of her life. However, he assured her that she would soon meet the person she was looking for. His reaction was too much for her to bear. She felt rejected and humiliated and shattered a glass vase she was holding against the tile floor. This is what her heart looked like now, she declared before storming out.

> **Every decision your heart makes has consequences.**

Months later she visited the church where she had met the man. As she entered, the pastor told her that someone had left a parcel for her at the church. He left to fetch it and returned with a fragile glass figurine in his hands. The craftsmanship was so delicate and masterly that it took her breath away. It was the most exquisite glasswork she had ever seen. Suddenly she realised that the glass figurine was made from the shards of the broken vase. In that moment, she understood that the pieces of her broken heart had been turned into something infinitely more beautiful than the original. Her heart had been re-created.

Sometimes our hearts also lie on the floor, shattered in a million pieces. They might even be crushed to powder. Fortunately, our Maker sees and picks up every tiny fragment and makes something spectacular out of it.

Your inner council

The different aspects of our being are like Derrick's directors sitting around the boardroom table. Those directors can illuminate the communication between the various aspects of our being and how they function. Just like real-life directors, these varying aspects have a shared goal – to create harmony and order. However, as with any company, the right order should be maintained. If you understand your inner council, you will also understand the decision-making process and behavioural choices better and be able to quickly identify inner turmoil. This becomes your motivation for change. Your heart is your inner council's managing director. The meaning of the Hebrew word for 'heart', leb, teaches us that the heart forms the nucleus of our being.

If every aspect of you plays its part, your whole being will experience inner harmony.

The heart should be able to make keen observations and interpret them correctly – much like a successful managing director. You must lead with your heart. When outsiders come knocking with advice, your heart must be able to discern and, if necessary, deny access. More on this in the last chapter.

Every decision your heart makes has consequences. If your heart becomes despondent as a result of recurring disappointment and disillusionment, passivity and inactivity soon follow. The heart loses confidence in its ability to direct the self – which is exactly what happened to Derrick. Eventually, exhaustion will cause the heart to abdicate its role as leader, leading to uncertainty and anxiety in the rest of you. Each aspect of the self will try to fill the heart's shoes, but that will only lead to greater chaos and uncertainty.

Soon, this lack of inner harmony will manifest in visible symptoms of a malfunctioning person: chronic fatigue, depression, majoring on minors (such as appearance), a weak immune system, and negative and/or manipulative relationships.

The stories in Part 1 have illustrated how mismanagement puts you on the road to nowhere. It keeps you from living with abandon. Every aspect of your being starts promoting its own agenda, which has a huge impact on the decision-making and general mood of your inner council. Their agendas correlate with the core questions each aspect of the self asks (see Chapter 8).

The body asks: 'What impact does this situation have on my survival?'

The spirit asks: 'Who is my God? What are my moral convictions about this situation? What influence will it have on my relationship with God?'

The heart asks: 'Who am I in this situation? What impact does it have on my self-definition?'

To know these answers, one needs to collect relevant information, welcome fresh data, and integrate insights that align with the revelation of your true worth (we'll discuss this in the next chapter). Our hearts yearn to truly know ourselves. To know – really know – the truth regarding your true worth and identity sets you up to handle and even celebrate the changes and challenges life throws at you. In John 16:32–33, Jesus speaks of the peace this knowledge brings:

Indeed the hour is coming, yes, has now come, that you will be scattered, each to his own, and will leave Me alone. And yet I am not alone, because the Father is with Me. These things I have spoken to you, that in Me you may have peace.

The knowledge that you are safely loved appoints peace as your legal guardian. A guardian controls who or what enters your gates. God's light will expose the lies that contradict the information you gained in this chapter. Consider this another step in reclaiming the ground that is part of your birthright.

The more secure you are in your understanding and acceptance of yourself, the less disturbance (incoherence) you will experience when conflicting data enters. This centredness will enhance your inner harmony (coherence) and consequently your social sphere. How you view *you* will ultimately influence how others view you and themselves. However, it starts with you.

The Pillar of Identity

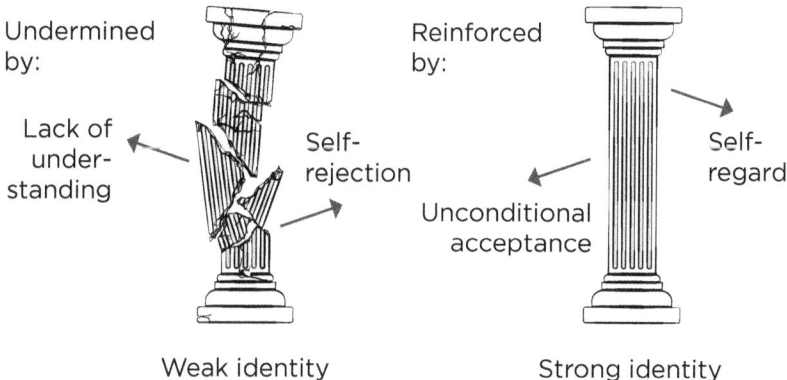

Undermined by:

Lack of under-standing

Self-rejection

Weak identity

Reinforced by:

Self-regard

Unconditional acceptance

Strong identity

We store our identity or self-definition in our hearts. It is the only place that allows us to give our raw, unvarnished opinion, regardless of what our moral convictions or relationship demands might be. We will ignore the convictions of our spirit (even if they are backed up by God's Word) if they clash with the beliefs we hold in our heart. Jesus taught the following (here recorded by Matthew):

> But those things which proceed out of the mouth come from the heart, and they defile a man.
>
> – MATTHEW 15:18

Your heart represents your deepest being. You are your heart.

The Heart-Centred Model

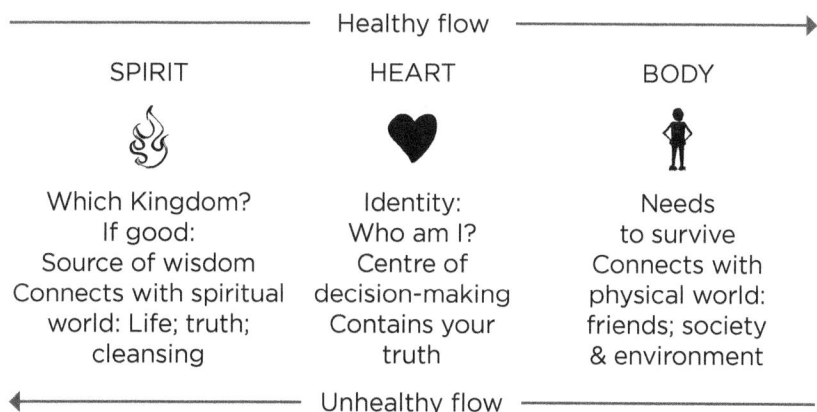

Healthy flow

SPIRIT	HEART	BODY
Which Kingdom? If good: Source of wisdom Connects with spiritual world: Life; truth; cleansing	Identity: Who am I? Centre of decision-making Contains your truth	Needs to survive Connects with physical world: friends; society & environment

Unhealthy flow

Derrick takes action

Self-love and self-acceptance play an enormous role. If your relationship with yourself is unhealthy, you will constantly struggle, no matter how many other sound relationships you have. Derrick will vouch for this.

Your attitude towards yourself, others, and life is radically altered by your broken heart. It also directly affects your relationship with God. Your attitude determines how you view yourself and others – God included – and what your posture (your '-ness') will be.

A broken heart's posture turns inward and asks: 'What about me?' Every situation and confrontation is perceived and interpreted as criticism or an insult. 'Everybody is against me.' 'Nobody cares.' 'I'm always the fly in the ointment.' Instead of moving away from negativity towards joy, such people throw anchor at self-pity, with bitterness and blame as their companions.

Over time such an attitude can poison your heart to such an extent that you view and experience the world with a very dark mindset indeed. Your behaviour becomes like that of the Israelites shortly after they left Egypt. They had seen God's power first-hand, but still longed for the fleshpots of Egypt every time they encountered the slightest obstacle. Blaming Moses and even God became a national pastime (see Exod 16:2–3).

Playing the blame game is a tell-tale sign of a broken heart or slave mentality, because it shows how exposed, powerless and full of self-pity you feel. Derrick felt hard done by the whole time. He focused on the injustice he had suffered, which blinded his heart to the way out. A slave mentality will keep you trapped in a victim mindset: 'I am a victim. Nothing is my fault. I will not take responsibility.' You keep focusing on someone else on whom you can blame your misfortune.

It is very easy to develop a victim mentality when we get hurt. The resulting inner chaos quickly spreads to our environment.

Chaos always makes us pine for order. A broken heart's pain can lead to efforts to create order through strict control. Often people who suffer will try to be someone else's saviour or redeemer. For the longest time, Derrick tried to control his team with threats and manipulation. He was convinced that he and only he would be able to save the company. A victim mentality and a saviour complex team up more often than you think. You think: I feel so exposed and powerless due to the injustice I have to suffer. I need some meaning in some aspect of my life. Meaning exorcises feelings of powerlessness and paralysis. The need for meaning drives you to make others dependent on you, so that you can feel in charge again. That is how you appropriate the role of saviour.

Often, the opposing attributes of such divergent roles and relationships present in the same person. In his relationship with his company, Derrick constantly wanted to be the saviour, but in his relationship with his wife, he was the suffering victim. Both these roles devastate the person and their environment, and the devastation further aggravates their anger.

It took a great deal of time before Derrick laid down his saviour mantle and surrendered to his feelings of anger and powerlessness. He was frustrated and angry. He felt boxed in and blamed those around him – Lydia, his business partner, and God – for feeling that way. 'Why did God allow that?' he asked me. 'How could Lydia do that to me?' But most of all, he was angry with himself. 'How could I have been so blind?' However, his biggest question remained the one he asked so reluctantly at our first meeting: 'Who am I, Derrick, in all of this?' His anger was fuelled by his fears, but his pride kept him from confronting these questions.

> **When you live from a heart that is whole, you move into the position God created you for.**

There was only one way out. Derrick's heart had to heal so that he could focus on God, the people around him, his company and his responsibilities again. In so doing, he would outgrow himself, see beyond his own needs and start serving others, thus making an impact on his environment.

Derrick started to understand where his responsibilities lay. He invited the best Counsellor to lead him with wisdom. With the Holy Spirit to guide him, he assumed his former position again, but this time without the pride he used to have. He apologised to his directors and assigned them to their proper positions once more. The confusion that reigned earlier was replaced with insight, respect, and order. This brave man forgave himself and the parties involved. He started to love himself again.

Through this whole process he slowly came to grips with who he was by looking at his own reflection in God's eyes. He was Derrick, a very precious person, created to be in a relationship with the living God!

Conclusion

A managing director who leads his team effectively, cares. That does not mean that he takes on more than his share of responsibility. On the contrary, it means that he acknowledges the diversity in his team and the potential harmony that could flow from that. He delegates work to everybody without feeling threatened and expects excellence from his employees. He encourages, mentors, equips, and respectfully admonishes. He does not issue threats. He does not manipulate. He does not try to control at all costs. He remains in charge and does not allow any third party to sow fear or worry in his company. Derrick managed to break out of his cramped 'cage' when he learned to forgive and love himself. His heart managed to breathe and heal once it was free from the shackles of bitterness and pride.

A heart that is whole is able to discern, lead, and humbly trust the One it invited in, the One who is called Wisdom. God's heart is full of compassion, humility, and gentleness (see Matt 11:29). Still, He is omnipotent. He has become Derrick's role model and inspiration. And the Holy Spirit is Derrick's Counsellor.

When you live from a heart that is whole, you move into the position God created you for. As Derrick worked through his hurt, he gradually moved into the right position, first in his inner council and later in his business. His relationships with himself, others, and his God and Saviour were restored. His heart was made whole. This enabled him to reclaim his identity and take up his rightful place with humility and joyful obedience to his Heavenly Father. The result was inner balance and unity among the different aspects of his self.

That is the condition for inner harmony. When you are there, the Source of life can constantly feed you and fill up your heart, so that you can channel his heart to your circle of influence. When you love and accept yourself in a healthy way, you grow to love others and especially your Creator God and Father.

When your heart experiences how He puts together the broken pieces, you look at the world with a grateful gaze. Gratitude and appreciation go hand in hand. Appreciation brings respect and humility. Each one helps to cultivate fertile soil, where the seeds of the Father's truth can take root and bear fruit.

MEDITATE A MOMENT

1. Think about a time when your heart was broken.
2. Who do you blame for that?
3. What effect did it have on you / does it still have on you?
4. Who do you blame for that?
5. Why?
6. What can you do about it? In other words: What about the situation lies within your power?
7. Why haven't you done it? What are you afraid of? What do you think will happen? What is your 'what if …'?
8. Does your heart have a strong connection to God's kingdom via your spirit? Do God's wisdom, insight, and discretion flow through to your heart?
9. How does your self-definition impact your world: relationships, behaviour, decisions, environment, and community?

Prayer

*Father, you are the King of kings. Today I want to declare
that You are also the King of my heart.
You do not focus on my outward appearance, but on my heart.
People only see what their eyes tell them, but Scripture tells us that
You look at the heart. Your Word says in 1 Kings 8:39 that You
alone know the hearts of all the sons of men. I stand before You
naked and exposed, Father. Please examine my heart and know me,
Lord. I so badly want a heart that is whole and healthy. Thank you
for assuring me that You will heal my heart and bring unity in my
inner being, but also unity with You and with your truth.
I want to experience inner harmony, Father.
I want to experience your peace in my heart and my whole being.
Father, in your refuge I want to lay bare my pain. I also want to
confess the sin and shame that entered my life because of it.
1 John 3:20 says You are greater than our heart that condemns us.
You know everything. I want to reiterate David's prayer in
verse 12 of Psalm 51: 'Create in me a clean heart, O God,
And renew a steadfast spirit within me.' Wash my heart in the blood
of Jesus, o Lord. I desire to have a heart that understands and
accepts, with integrity, its position and responsibilities
as chairperson of my inner council.
Please give me a sincere heart.
I want to live a life of impact, Father. Enable me through your
Holy Spirit to inspire hope in other people's hearts.
Remind me of the things that confuse, mislead and betray my heart,
and show me how to fix them with the help of your Holy Spirit.
I want to focus my heart's attention on You and search for You with
all my heart. Teach me your ways, so that I might walk in your
truth. Teach my heart to fear your Name.
You are my great Enabler, King of my heart. I gladly embark
on this journey of re-creation with You.
In the Name of Jesus, my Saviour, and to your glory.
Amen.*

---

1. Modulation of DNA Conformation by Heart-Focused Intention, Rollin McCraty PhD, Mike Atkinson and Dana Tomasino.
2. At the Fels Research Institute in Ohio, USA.

CHAPTER 11

CHANGE

Four steps of change

Catalysts speed up or delay reactions without being changed or consumed by the reactions themselves. Of necessity, we depend on certain catalysts to keep us moving as time passes. The secret is to discern between the life catalysts that enable us to grow and move forward, and those that lead to regression. The former we should embrace; the latter we should avoid at all costs.

A hunger for eternity

Temporary things only last for a while. They quickly pass. Every temporary change potentially brings new expectations and new disappointments. Disappointment hinders your hope and weakens your faith. It exhausts you. It wrecks your trust and belief, and wastes precious time.

As people of the heart, we hunger and thirst for things that have eternal value. Unfortunately, the passage of time and the vagaries of life wear down this appetite.

Let's quickly recap what we have covered so far: Every experience penetrates our being and influences our inner world. To process each experience requires a complex-yet-fascinating process that necessitates cooperation between body, spirit, and heart. Each of these aspects of our being has a contribution to make, but when one or more of them starts functioning outside its role or rank, it disturbs our inner harmony and limits our capacity for God's truth. What follows is often misinterpretation of sensory data and the development of a false narrative. In turn, this leads to increasingly desperate attempts to make sense of the world, which only leads to further disappointment and frustration. How do we break this vicious cycle?

Can frustration be a good thing?

To get where you want to be from your current position takes energy. One of the names for that type of energy is frustration. You do not want to stay where you are, in other words you are frustrated with your position. This frustration energy can be spent in two ways: You can either use it in a way that adds to your despair and powerlessness, making you ever more angry or depressed. Or you can use it as motivation to reach your goal. Frustration harnessed as motivation mobilises your will.

My dad used to doodle on restaurant serviettes if he wanted to communicate one of his philosophies or enlighten me about some topic. The things that he shared with such excitement at that stage of his life have become precious keepsakes. In one of his serviette sketches, he explained the frustration principle, which I proudly present to you:

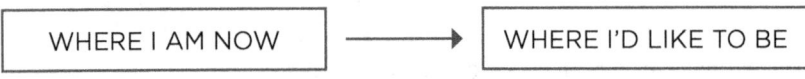

WHERE I AM NOW ⟶ WHERE I'D LIKE TO BE

FRUSTRATION ENERGY

The farther apart the two points, the bigger your frustration. Frustration breeds desperation. This begs the question: Where will this desperation ultimately lead you?

Your choice in the matter will determine that. You can use the energy for cultivating self-pity and a slave mentality, or you can use it to kick-start the required process of change.

Motivation brings momentum

From your earliest days you have had needs, some of them non-negotiable. Over time your needs change, but one thing remains the same: The intensity of your needs will determine your motivation. In other words, the depth of your desire to get away from, or to reach, a specific place determines your desperation.

Ask yourself some key questions: What determines your desire? What are you hungry and thirsty for? In other words, why do you want to reach your desired destination so badly? Why do you want to break free from your current existence? This 'why energy' is your motivation.

DESIRED ITEM/POSITION + DESPERATION = MOTIVATION

OR

SITUATION I'D LIKE TO ESCAPE + DESPERATION
= MOTIVATION

Ties of love and fear influence your thinking and choices, and play a big role in your motivation. When your ties with others (and with yourself) are mainly ties of love, your motivation will likely lead you to your desired destination without fear and worry plaguing you with thoughts of failure and disappointment. You will know that reaching your goal won't add to your personal worth, therefore you won't fear rejection. However, when your relationships are laced with fear, fear of rejection becomes your primary driver. You want to avoid that at all costs.

Gates and locks that open and close

As we move through the day, we are constantly bombarded with information. The things you see, hear, smell, taste, feel, and sense enter your body with – or sometimes without – your knowledge or express consent. Your senses are like portals or gateways for the bits of data in your environment. There are other portals too (see previous chapter), but let's focus on the sensory ones for now. Outside information is carried into and through your body, from neuron to neuron, in an electrical and chemical manner. Read more about this fascinating process in Addendum A.

What you do with this stream of information depends on quite a number of things. How you handle it shows how you interpret the world around you and how you assimilate it into your inner world. The way you process messages and view the world gives a good indication of what your inner alignment looks like.

From birth, our nerve cells are poised to make connections to other nerve cells. The more you are stimulated by outside information, the more connections are formed between your nerve cells. Usually, the information is divided into association groups – according to type, that is. One of the unintended consequences of this is the brain's tendency to generalise. Let's look at the way we process information and the potential deception this can cause:

For one neuron (nerve cell) to send a message to another, there must be a difference in their electrical charge. The right charge differential between the inner and outer membrane of the axon enables the electrical impulses to carry the message to the end of the nerve cell. Potassium (K^+) and Sodium (Na^+) play an important role in getting an adequate electrical charge, since they cause a charge differential between the inside and outside, down the length of the axon (see sketch below). The passing along of messages is directly affected by this process. This charge differential brings about an *action potential*. (Addendum A discusses this process in more detail.)

An action potential is needed to convey the message by way of an impulse, and to pass it on to the next receiver neuron.

To achieve the desired action potential (so that the message may be relayed effectively), a few things need to be in place.

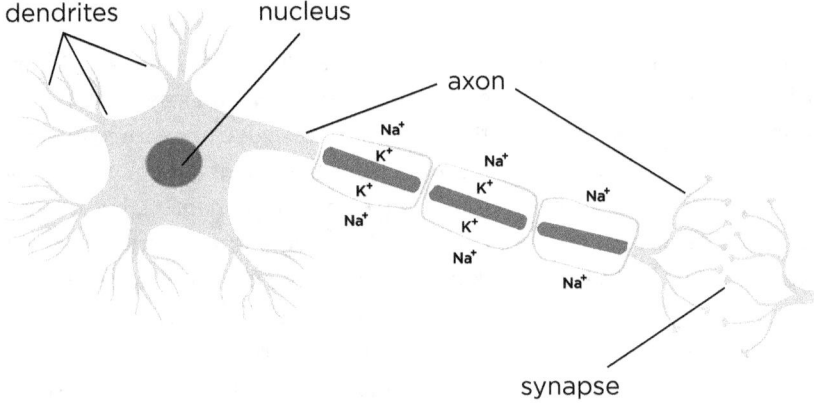

Potassium and Sodium play an important role in bringing about an action potential.

Genetic filtration

All incoming information is potentially important. However, since approximately 10 million bits of data from the environment enter your brain every second, a filter is definitely needed. About 99% of the incoming information from the spine is filtered by a dense network of nerve fibres. Even finer filtration happens in the brain, inside the neurons themselves.

As we mentioned earlier, this filtration only takes place through a complex process. Determining how the incoming information should be handled is an urgent matter. The best path for relaying the message is chosen so that interpretation, behavioural, and processing choices can happen, and that lasting connections can be made.

All incoming information is therefore sorted by rank, but how are ranks assigned? Who determines what information takes precedence? Usually, fresh information that can be grouped with older, similar data gets tagged as high priority. Previous experiences therefore have a huge influence on the importance attached to information. Anne's story is a good illustration of how this process works.

There are three situations in which incoming information soars straight to the highest rank and gets processed without any alterations. More about that later.

When information reaches the neuron filters, the process of genetic interpretation automatically kicks into gear. The filter you use when you have to channel incoming information, consists of hereditary data (that you 'inherited' along with your genes) and the beliefs you have formed through experience. That filter determines whether you will accept the information, ignore, it or adapt it to your existing beliefs. These choices are made in the nuclei of your neurons. The genetic filter thus determines how you handle data.

The detail of this filtration process and the interpretation of information will be discussed in Addendum B. It is fascinating to read how the composition of your DNA is involved with the formation of specific proteins for the content of the message.

Anne

'I never said that you're not allowed to have a boyfriend, Anne!' Her dad was at his wits' end. Sitting with his elbows on his knees, he had his head in his hands. He felt as if his words reached his daughter all twisted. The communication between father and daughter had somehow evaporated, and he had no clue how to go about restoring her trust.

Frank and Adele got divorced some three years ago, and both

of them tried to make the process as amicable as possible. Their only daughter, Anne, saw her dad on alternate weekends and every other holiday.

He did not have a clue what was going on in her life. The only explanation he could think of was that his daughter had women's issues that were beyond his understanding. He tried talking to Adele about it, but his ex-wife always took it personally, which only served to set off the old, exhausting cycle of destructive, draining communication. Consequently, Frank has learned to keep his observations to himself.

Anne slammed her bedroom door. It was testimony to the quality of the builders' craftsmanship that the door remained attached to the hinges, Frank thought, and poured himself another whiskey.

His daughter's puzzling behaviour started after the divorce. Every time he saw her, he could sense how she was increasingly drawing away from him. As if he was the villain who had been responsible for the whole divorce. What bothered him most, was that her spontaneity, her joy, and her infectious laugh had disappeared almost completely. It had always been part of her, but now it was lacking altogether.

That was when Frank called me. He gave me some background over the phone, and we set an appointment for Anne. Her reluctance to see me the first day was crystal clear. If she had dragged her feet any more, there would be two furrows on the floor of my practice. She sat on the front edge of the couch and stroked my dog to give herself something to do. Her eyes avoided mine and she shrouded her inner being with an invisible blanket.

Change needs to happen at heart level if you want to experience lasting renewal.

Anne's story slowly unfolded and little by little she allowed me into the darkness she felt inside her. She was afraid. Afraid of disappointing her parents and afraid that nobody would be able to pull her from the pit she was in. What if she remained there … permanently?

Unfortunately, this beautiful young girl's story is not unique. She had met Juan at a friend's place one evening. He ran with the cool crowd, had an enormous Instagram following and self-confidence to spare. Anne was only too grateful when he showed interest in her, but she quickly became entangled in a web of abuse and confusion – a victim like so many other insecure young girls around the world. When messages and pictures of your 'love' is disseminated through various social media channels, it becomes the property of a vast and terribly unstable community. Juan had promised that it would be for his eyes only, but his words rang hollow and his respect for her was just an illusion. It was a deadly web out of which she could not escape without humiliation leaving some serious scars.

Anne told her story of abuse. Social media had exposed her most private and intimate self. The Anne of a few months prior would never return. Her innocence, her sincere trust in people, and the dreams she dreamed had been ripped from her.

'Describe your dad to me, Anne. What is he to you?' I probed.

'He's never there for me. He doesn't care what becomes of me,' she said, reaching for some tissues to dry her tears.

'And your mother?'

Anne laughed cynically. 'My mom is just trying to survive. I do not think she'll even realise if I'm not there.' She looked down at the tissue she was clutching. 'It's not that she doesn't love me. It's just that my dad pulled the rug from under her when he left.' She looked up, the reproving anger back in her eyes. 'He basically discarded us both like trash.'

'Where does your parents' divorce leave you, Anne?' I asked gently. 'On an island all alone. As in utterly, utterly alone.'

Isolation is life-threatening

Anne's feeling of being deserted stretched far back. After her birth, her mom, Adele, fell into such postpartum depression that she had to be admitted to hospital a few times. A babysitter looked after Anne while her dad used his demanding job as a form of escape. The emotional problems of the females in his household left Frank feeling completely helpless and unqualified.

Adele's depression had far-reaching consequences, among which were a poor self-image and a lack of support to her daughter. So, from a young age, Anne had to try and make sense of the world on her own. Her dad's news that he wanted a divorce only added to her feelings of rejection.

> **Rewriting your heart's truth comprises four basic steps: becoming aware, recognising, understanding, and turning.**

What will become of me? Who will look after me? Who would want me? These questions raised Anne's desperate need to be included and to feel accepted in her community to dangerous levels. Juan appeared on the scene like a knight in shining armour. His attention was like manna from heaven to Anne. *Surely, if someone like Juan wants me, I can't be that bad?* Juan was like a spider sitting next to his web, waiting for his prey. To disentangle yourself from such a web requires redefinition and, especially, reconstruction of your inner pathways. A new reality had to be etched on the tablets of her heart.

The process of change

To embark on a journey of restoration like Anne, you need a firm grasp on the process to change. We will discuss each phase of this process in greater detail. Look at the diagram below. In short, the process looks as follows:

1. AT THE START
• Remember, we all have different opinions and assumptions about life. • Day-to-day experiences confirm or confront these beliefs about your life, people, yourself, and God. • Every bit of data that travels from your senses, needs to be processed in some or other way. • There are mainly three ways in which incoming information can be processed. • To change, you must really want to change. This decision will supply the energy to investigate your established way of handling situations.
2. MOVING FORWARD
• When you've gained insight about how you normally process information, a desire to change will (hopefully) develop. • Changing your existing interpretations requires adaptation and the rewriting of your current beliefs (your truth). • *This change needs to happen at heart level if you want to experience lasting renewal.*

2. MOVING FORWARD (CONTINUED)
• A change of heart will manifest at a spiritual, physical, and chemical level.
• New experiences and fresh information with sufficient action potential will penetrate right down to your heart.
• Any incoming data will either confirm your existing beliefs at a heart level or expose them as potentially flawed.
3. PENETRATION OF MESSAGES
• We will look at three opportunities when new / fresh data (i.e. data that clashes with previous information) will reach / penetrate the heart level.
• When that happens, your heart's truth is rewritten.
• This new truth or reality may or may not coincide with God's truth.
• Two of the three circumstances where new data rewrites your heart's truth can happen without direct divine revelation, although it can still correspond with God's truth.
• The third circumstance only happens when God Himself reveals his truth to you through first-hand experience.
• Such an encounter replaces your truth with God's truth.
• That is when re-creation takes place.
• Rewriting your heart's truth comprises four basic steps: becoming aware, recognising, understanding, and turning (see p. 180–189).

You need to fundamentally understand each step if you'd like to follow them closely. Anne's journey of re-creation illustrates this process and will encourage every person that ever felt like her. Her example teaches us that change is indeed possible.

Why do I need to change?

That is a good question. Sometimes people are prepared to put in the work because they really *want* to change. However, change can also come about through events and circumstances that are completely unplanned and out of our control. We can't plan for these eventualities. Sometimes life just happens. Such events can change – and even warp – the way we see ourselves, others, and God.

However, when you realise that your experience-based truth does not necessarily correspond to the truth of the Word, hopefully you will start looking for change and re-creation. When you find that you are deceived by half-truths and subjective assumptions, or if you find yourself in a dark place, longing for relief, you *want* to change.

When you stand in front of a mirror, your reflection stares back at you. When the mirror is warped, your reflection is not a true representation of what you look like. In the same way, your self-definition will be skewed if you base it on other people's disrespectful or dismissive behaviour towards you. Parents' behaviour towards their children leaves an indelible impression. Neither Adele with her postpartum depression nor Frank with the divorce proceedings intended to reject their daughter, but their choices and behaviour held up a warped mirror in front of her. She felt unworthy, unloved, and utterly alone.

Fortunately, Anne's increasing isolation (emotional distancing) from her family set off the alarm bells in Frank's head. Her quiet, subdued, and withdrawn behaviour was far removed from that of the daughter he used to know. Even so, she did not reach out for help. She had to reach the point of desperation first. The gap between where she was and where she wanted to be had to be defined and broken down for her. Hope needed to spring in her heart that change was possible.

Since Anne did not come to me of her own accord, I had to guide her along the path of discovery very respectfully. Her journey made her see how she viewed the world and interpreted people's behaviour. Gradually, all manners of deception started to show themselves. After Anne recognised her negative behaviour patterns, she acknowledged her need to change.

Four stops on the road to discovery

Sensory data that flows from your senses to your brain goes through specific processes. One can write several volumes about the different stages of processing, but an abridged version will do for our purpose. When sensory data enters your brain with lots of energy, it requires focus and attention. You have to make up your mind how you will process this information: with care and focus, or only glancingly. If the message does require concentration due to its high energy level (electrical charge), it will be processed more urgently than usual.

Data is processed as follows:

1. An incident occurs.
2. Sensory data streams into your system and is interpreted by your personal genetic filter.
3. A processing path is laid out and the data gets processed, usually according to your established interpretations.
4. Next, you execute your chosen behaviour.

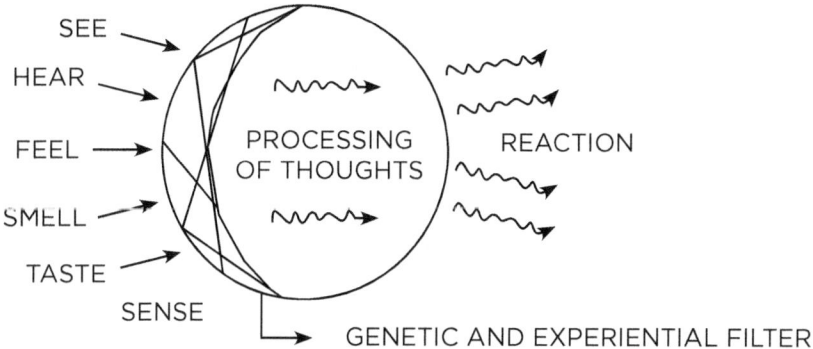

SEE
HEAR
FEEL
SMELL
TASTE
SENSE

PROCESSING OF THOUGHTS

REACTION

GENETIC AND EXPERIENTIAL FILTER

The whole process takes split seconds. You will likely only become aware of the incident's impact once you have reacted.

Anne's willingness to succumb to Juan's demands confused her and made her feel ashamed. It drove her further away from her parents. In turn, her parents felt confused and concerned every time she withdrew and beat herself up for long periods of time. Processing's first stop typically looks like this: Messages are conveyed, but are interpreted differently by the respective parties. An incident can act as a trigger, that "something" that sets off the first domino in your neuron arrangement.

One of Anne's triggers was looking into Juan's piercing eyes. It made her succumb to his manipulation time and again. An hour or so later her reaction would leave her dumbfounded, confused, and ashamed. Her feelings of isolation and loneliness grew every time. Her opinion of herself, others, and God was also affected by this.

> If you want to decipher your heart's
> language, pay close attention
> to your behaviour.

A trigger starts the process of interpretation. After that, you filter the information and decide how you want to process it – that is the second stop. You can leave it unchanged or adapt it to fit your established, familiar convictions. Your filter is mainly formed through previous experiences of, say, rejection, self-pity, or distrust.

People mostly choose the path of least resistance. You will too when new data reaches your brain. Your body instinctively wants to conserve energy, so you interpret incoming data (like the trigger) according to your old beliefs and associations. When fresh information differs from your deeply held convictions, it requires considerably more energy. More about this later.

The third stop is the processing of your interpretation so that you can choose an appropriate course of action. Your old beliefs are like well-travelled highways – easy to follow. They represent your established convictions, i.e. your truth that is based on your personal processing of the data. Your first instinct is to believe your old assumptions.

Previous experience plays a big part in this. Our natural tendency is to confirm what we 'know' as 'true'. *I knew it! I told you so!*' Your convictions reveal your heart's opinion about the definition of truth. Your truth becomes evident through filtering, processing, and ultimately through the choices you make.

> **If you want to reign, you need to position yourself correctly.**

The fourth stop is where your body takes over and executes your decision. This, more than anything else, reveal your deepest convictions. If you want to decipher your heart's language, pay close attention to your behaviour. From time to time, one has to press pause, sit back, and replay incidents in your mind so that you can observe them properly.

You also need to ask yourself some important questions: What caused this behaviour or reaction? (What really happened?) What was the trigger? Why does the trigger affect me in this way? You can even write down the answers.

Change does not happen by trying to change or avoid the triggers. Sustained change is brought about by forming new associations with your triggers. Your circumstances might never change, but their impact on you can change dramatically. You (including your choices, behaviour, and convictions) cannot afford to be controlled by your circumstances. You were created to rule, not to be ruled over. If you want to reign, you need to position yourself correctly.

Once Anne got to know what her triggers were and how they influenced her, she was able to get the process of change going. When you realise that your behaviour does not mesh with your faith or with God's truth, the necessity of change presents itself to you.

These four steps indicate what your heart's convictions are. Are they in line with your experience and your interpretation, or are they in line with God's truth? Are you living your truth, or his truth?

The answers to these questions create a hunger in you to change and to be re-created so that your truth may be replaced by the truth of your Saviour and God the Father.

After Anne had travelled this road to discovery, her answer to the question 'Do you want to change?' was a resounding 'Yes!'.

You yourself maintain your truth

When you are confronted by data that contradicts your heart's convictions, you have three options:

1. Ignore the data and do not involve higher cognition (consideration, analysis, and decision-making).
2. Tweak the data to suit your existing convictions.
3. Accommodate the new data as is and adapt your convictions (your truth) to the new information.

Every day every human being processes thousands of bits of information without involving higher cognition. Your system is bombarded with data and you have to choose how to handle it. This process mostly takes place automatically, almost subconsciously. It is only when information requires your attention that you have to choose between the second and third option above. Also keep the action potential in mind.

When Anne's dad told her that he was worried about her (and the friend she saw), her filter interpreted the information as criticism and disapproval. Her sensory data's filter was called rejection. She interpreted his commentary in line with her well-worn, familiar neural pathways. She chose option two, deciding: *My dad does not want me to be happy. He does not really care for me. He just does not want me to have a boyfriend.*

Her experience of rejection when he moved out, leaving her alone with her absent mother, reinforced this filter and broadened that particular pathway of her truth. *Nobody really cares for me. I have to fend for myself.*

The second option of processing takes place without much effort. Suppose your typical, most familiar experiences originate in messages of rejection (let's call them triangle messages or ▲ messages). If you regularly receive such messages, your brain will develop established paths and receptors that will not only accommodate these messages, but seek such stimuli out for confirmation's sake. Processing of ▲ messages happens fast and does not require a great deal of energy.

When Anne does experience inclusion and acceptance, she suddenly receives a strange, new message (let's call them ■ messages). She does not have ■ receptors for the ■ message, and it does not fit her ▲ receptors either.

For example, one of Anne's friends invited her to spend a weekend with her on their family farm. The two girls had met after school and immediately 'clicked'. Anne, however, was suspicious about the reason for the invite. Her exclusion filter caused her to view a simple gesture of friendship with overmuch caution.

The new ■ message did not confirm her conviction that nobody cares. When Anne's friend told her how much she liked her, the words were like invaders, confronting the inner picture Anne held. It was a strange message (a ■ message) that could not readily be accepted by her established ▲ receptors. Processing of new messages requires a conscious decision (and extra energy).

Sometimes we choose the third processing option involuntarily. A recurring message or an experience that is accompanied by lots of emotion can change your heart's truth, even if you did not consciously ask for it. Your brain will go to great lengths to produce sufficient protein for adequate chemical structures to process such messages comprehensively. (There is also a third type of message that causes your heart's truth to adapt, but we will discuss it later.)

> **The psyche has to metabolise trauma –
> break it up into bite-size pieces that
> your system can handle.**

However, you will likely process new messages according to the first two options subconsciously before your heart has had time to make room for a new truth. Since childhood, the message from Anne's inner pathways (her truth) was that she had to survive on her own. Her mom's depression and emotional unavailability, and her dad taking refuge in work made it impossible for Anne to construct the pathways she needed. There were no pathways to convince her that she was worthy of her parents' time and attention. Her interpretation, cemented in her neural pathways, confirmed this conviction. She acted to protect her truth.

How does change take place?

As we saw earlier, messages only travel between neurons if there is a sufficient charge differential. It is as if your body says: *OK, fine. I'll accommodate this data.* Let's investigate the way new messages confront and rebuild your neural pathways in greater detail. When you choose to change your thoughts to the point of changing your being, like Anne did, the following aspects are very important.

The high energy required for passing on message impulses can be brought about in three ways:

- Strong emotion
- Repetition
- The sword of God's Word

Let's quickly discuss the first two possibilities before we look at the third in greater detail.

Strong emotion

During an emotional experience, the stimulus will be strong enough to ensure that the message gets sent along. The message is accepted without any adaptation, even though it seems strange (i.e. atypical or completely new). If the emotion is caused by trauma, it is likely that you will separate the raw facts (what actually transpired) from the emotion and suppress those facts until you are able to process it little by little.

The psyche has to metabolise trauma – break it up into bite-size pieces that your system can handle, so that your psyche can digest it piece by piece until you have assimilated the trauma and incorporated it into your view of how life works. You can even benefit from your trauma, as we will learn in the next chapter.

A big birthday party, wedding, or achievement is celebrated and processed with a lot of positive emotion. How can you ever forget your wedding day or the days on which your children were born? These great experiences are permanently etched onto the tables of your heart.

Extremely positive and extremely negative emotions penetrate deeply as a result of our respect for the message. Your brain pays attention to such emotionally charged impulses and processes it with the required respect. The important role that emotion plays in cementing our memories has been proven by thorough research.[1] The researchers found that emotionally charged events are remembered more clearly than neutral ones. According to the research leader, Dr Luis Fuentemilla, emotions were a direct portal to memory formation.

Repetition

During consolidation (when events are recorded to form long-term memories), repetition is one of the strongest components. Research has shown that babies develop a rudimentary vocabulary in the womb already. If the mother communicates her actions and stories repeatedly (more than three times) to her unborn baby in word or song, postnatal tests have shown visible brain activity that indicates recognition.

Repetition brings about the attention energy required for the accommodation and direct processing of data. It happens gradually, but usually my clients are buoyed by this truth, not discouraged. You remain in control while you repeat certain truths to yourself. Michael, the guy who struggled with porn addiction who had to 'work on his faith', initially relied heavily on this.

Repetition or memorisation of the Word can be extremely efficient, as long as you work through the other mobilising conditions too and till the soil of your heart, so that the Word may find it fertile and receptive. If not, it will remain an intellectual exercise, with little to no 'heart'.

The double-edged sword

The active role of the Word in our lives is one gift that God in his infinite mercy gave us to bring about change that lasts for eternity. He is our Re-Creator. His Spirit manifests the work of Jesus Christ in our whole being – body, heart and spirit. God re-creates the whole person – the soul person.

> For the word of God *is* living and powerful, and sharper than any two-edged sword, piercing even to the division of soul and spirit, and of joints and marrow, and is a discerner of the thoughts and intents of the heart.
>
> – HEBREWS 4:12

The impact of God's Word is the third component that will accommodate incoming data that runs counter to established beliefs. If you do not welcome input from this source of eternal truth, your own truth (old convictions) will forever be running the show called your life. Your heart's truth will continue to dominate your decisions and behaviour patterns.

When your truth differs from God's truth, you need a double-edged incision by the Word so that God's truth can pierce your heart and bring about change that sets you up for eternity. You can compare the Word to seed that is planted in the soil of your heart. In Luke 8:15 Jesus tells his disciples:

> 'But the ones [seeds] *that* fell on the good ground are those who, having heard the word with a noble and good heart, keep *it* and bear fruit with patience.'

Anne experienced the Word's powerful impact. As her confidence grew, God's truth started to become firmly established in her life. The most valuable truths that brought her a breakthrough were the ones about who she really was, why she had worth and who her Saviour was.

His Word, sharper than any double-edged sword, pierces even to the division of soul and spirit, and of joints and marrow. The Word penetrates the portals of our senses, enters the gate of our spirit and cuts accurately through our soul and spirit, to the very core of our being. (Re-read Chapter 1 for more about this surgical intervention.)

We can illustrate the process as follows:

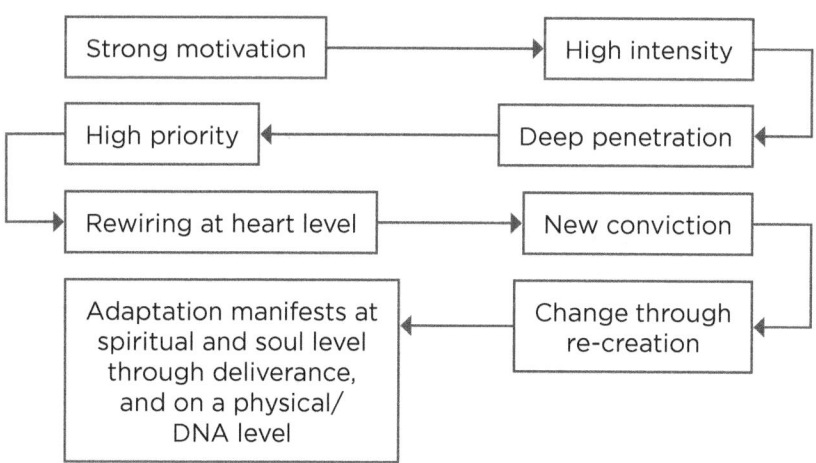

Long-term change comes from a changed heart. The change potential that initially starts from the outside or reaches up from your spirit, reaches your psyche's core – your heart, the true you. It goes all the way to your seat of power and authority. When you fill the core of your being with God's liberating truth, He re-creates the control centre of your whole existence.

But how does this piercing happen? What part do you play in the process? What should you do to make this change happen at heart level? Moses's heart cry was to know God better. 'Show me now your way, that I may know You and that I may find grace in your sight,' he prays in Exodus 33:13. The Hebrew word that is translated with 'know' in this verse refers to a whole process of growth and change. One could paraphrase this verse as follows: *May I gradually become more deeply and intimately acquainted with who You are by focusing on You, acknowledging You and understanding You better.*

Acquiring this life-changing knowledge of God comes about through four steps: becoming aware, recognising, understanding, and turning. These four steps also form the basis for long-term (eternal) change.

Jesus said:

For the hearts of this people have grown dull.
Their ears are hard of hearing,
And their eyes they have closed,
Lest they should see with *their* eyes and hear with *their* ears,
Lest they should understand with *their* hearts and turn,
So that I should heal them.
– MATTHEW 13:15

A proud heart can rob your senses of godly truth.

Step 1: Becoming aware – to truly hear and see

Intentionally hearing and seeing enable you to recognise and process information, and to produce an appropriate response from deep inside you. To listen and to behold, turn your heart's attention towards the source. Attentive hearts allow new information, whether visual or audible, to reshape them. Just like the good soil Jesus described in the gospels, attentive hearts provide good soil in which new seed can send down roots, grow and produce a bountiful harvest.

Change is the fruit that proves that you successfully negotiated the journey from perceiving Truth to turning towards it. That is change on a heart level. That is true transformation.

Your eyes and ears are your main conduits of information. Along with your invisible senses, they play a pivotal role in the process of change. Let us take a look at these remarkable, God-given tools for perceiving truth.

To hear

The *Shema* (Hebrew for the exhortative 'Hear!') is the Jewish confession of faith that starts with Deuteronomy 6:4: 'Hear, O Israel: The LORD our God, the LORD is one!' God wants you to listen. Your listening ability depends in part on the information you allow access to. Keep in mind that your heart carries your deepest convictions. Those beliefs filter what you hear. They act as your ear's guardian and set the baseline for what sounds acceptable and what does not. Your baseline is your default way of perceiving, the one you're familiar with. *You listen with your heart.*

How you listen determines how you choose. Your choices determine your behaviour. Your behaviour reveals your truth.

How does this filter work? It is an important question that can be answered by taking a closer look at our primary hearing organ.

The physical ear helps us to understand the function of the unseen ear. It consists of the most fascinating and complex systems. According to a professor in otolaryngology, neurology, as well as hearing and speech at Vanderbilt University in Tennessee, there are more nerve tendrils in the ear per square centimetre than anywhere else in the body.

Sound travels at a speed of more than 343 metres per second, i.e. 1 236 kilometres per hour. Sound reaches the ear via one of two routes, a short one and a longer one. Route 2 is on average 66 millimetres longer, which brings about a 0,2-millisecond time difference. Your brain therefore receives no fewer than four sound feeds, which helps you to discern a lot of detail.

The location of your ears on the side of your head helps you to pinpoint the source of the sound accurately. Once we determine the source, we place a predetermined value on it. Is it trustworthy? If so, we afford it respect, first-grade processing, and a high likelihood of integration. If not, it might not even enjoy higher cognitive evaluation and be disregarded.

It requires a high level of regard for a source to escalate the act of listening to the act of acknowledging, processing, and integrating its information. If that level is reached and the source is accommodated, it will flow into behaviour that acknowledges the information as truth.

However, the ear can be deceived, listen only selectively and ignore information in favour of existing beliefs, regardless of how true it is.

When our ears have been damaged by loud music or other high-decibel noise (anything over 90 dB), we tend to fill in the gaps. It is easy to slip into selective listening when we are forced to listen to someone or find ourselves bored by a speech or a tedious story.

Listening is vital for true transformation.

Connecting words like we connect dots is something we all do. When people tell us something, it is easy to default to listening with half an ear and simply fill in the gaps ourselves. In fact, our filters actively support this. It saves energy. Or so we think. The aforementioned hearing loss may not be the main reason why stories get personalised, but it does account for some of it.

According to studies, almost 48 million people in America alone suffer from hearing loss. That is a big number of ears that can't listen properly.

How does that affect follow-through on the content we hear? It is daunting to think that effective listening almost always requires a form of response and change – in the person who listens as well as the person who talks.

Listening is a dying art, because so many of us have developed filters to cope with the demanding flow of information that bombards us. How can we tune our ears to discern the truth amid so much noise?

The art of listening

In her book *You Are Not Listening*, Kate Murphy discusses how crucial listening is in our daily lives – in every relationship, whether it is marriage, parenting, work, charity, or politics. In times of war or illness, your ability to listen can literally mean the difference between life and death. Families are torn apart, because partners have lost the willingness to listen to each other's heart. We are all running earnestly on the treadmill of life, desperately attempting to meet its unreasonable – and often unnecessary – demands.

According to studies done by Microsoft, the average attention span has shrunk from 12 seconds to 8, resulting in marketing and entertainment that grows ever more cryptic. Murphy rightly states: 'We are participating in an attention economy.'

That does not change the fact that listening is vital for true transformation. For starters, hearing builds our faith:

> So faith comes from hearing, that is, hearing the Good News about Christ.
>
> – Romans 10:17 NLT

You listen selectively. You are predisposed to tune in to a certain wavelength.

To be skilled in the art of listening is, however, a vital key in true transformation. It involves cutting through the overwhelming cacophony of sound with a heart that is eagerly focused on hearing one thing only: God's voice, the sound of truth. That is how we gain understanding and faith.

When your heart turns like a satellite dish to focus on the Source of truth, the ears of your heart will be opened. You will listen like never before, mobilising your whole being to follow through on the things you hear. Listening will lead to obedience. This is love in action.

Listen, therefore, with your whole heart:

> '… they might see with their eyes, hear with their ears, understand with their hearts, and turn and be healed.'
>
> – Isaiah 6:10 NIV

To see

The other gateway that provides information for potential change is the eyes, also called the windows of your soul. The nature of the information you allow to enter through your 'windows' is, of course, very important.

Your gaze creates room for impressions. Your gaze forms a wide-open space for your inner being to dance and perform somersaults to your heart's delight.

However, you can look without *seeing*. You can watch but still deny full access to the object you are watching. But if you watch because you *want* to see, the image is allowed in to tinker with your inner world. Your gaze changes into sight and enjoys your full attention.

So how do we look to really see?

At the base of the brain, one finds the pineal gland that produces the sleep hormone melatonin. Melatonin and the hypothalamus combine to regulate your sleeping and waking hours. The hypothalamus serves as your body clock.

The pineal gland is light-sensitive, which shows in the cyclical nature of the way it works. Scientists have observed 24-hour cycles in the body's serotonin and melatonin concentrations. Both these hormones play an important part in our daily functioning and mood management. More importantly, they enable us to focus and concentrate. Serotonin is produced in the intestine (gut-brain) and the pineal gland. In the latter, it is also transformed into melatonin.

> **Meditation is focusing and concentrating on God, his Word and his truth.**

Meditation involves a singular focus and looking beyond the physical. Such a gaze approximates an invitation. It opens you up and prepares you for input. Unfortunately, many people reject meditation because they attach negative connotations to it. However, meditation can be a worthwhile aid on the healing journey. It teaches you to see afresh, to gaze through the eyes of your heart for the purpose of seeing, knowing, and growing your understanding.

Fascinating research shows that meditation has a direct influence on the hypothalamus and the pineal gland. Use of the hallucinogenic drug LSD (which has a similar chemical structure to that of melatonin) as well as deep meditation cause the pineal gland to produce less melatonin and serotonin. That makes certain areas of the brain very impressionable, especially the parts where not many neural pathways have formed. These parts, which often lie in the right brain (the creative side), are like the pages of a new notebook yearning for ink.

We are very susceptible to new suggestions when we are in a state of meditation. We tend to allow access to new data with much less prejudice when we meditate, regardless of whether such data is true or dangerously misleading. Logical thought does not interfere with the suggestions presented to you at that stage. This is dangerous if you are tripping on LSD or putting yourself into a trance state, but it is great if you are focusing on God's truth. Fresh truth can penetrate deeply without your old arguments and beliefs getting in the way.

To be clear, the meditation to which I refer is focusing and concentrating on God, his Word and his truth. It means that your eyes are fixed on Him and Him alone, that you desire to truly know Him as your God, and that you adopt his truth as your own. It means that you long to be united with Him.

This type of 'seeing' never fails to elicit reaction from your Saviour. In fact, He promises it. In Matthew 7:7, Jesus says: 'Seek, and you will find.' In David's last instructions to his son Solomon, he says: 'If you seek Him, He will be found by you' (1 Chron 28:9). Then you will love Him with all your heart (see Matt 22:37).

When you look and really see, your heart opens up to God's input. It prepares you for the treasures He'd like to share with you, writing them on the tablet of your heart. It is a gaze full of trust. The more you trust, the more spontaneously you allow his words and his light into your life. Light brings revelation and recognition of what is his and what you haven't surrendered yet.

Your way of seeing is the starting point in God's process of change. Your focus causes his Word and his truth to penetrate your heart, even if it does not correspond with your own truth. Without it, you will struggle to get established in his truth.

Step 2: Recognising – to welcome light and sound

The older you get, the more knowledge you accumulate. Usually, this knowledge is filed according to our associations. Your knowledge of the Word increases in the same way. You study the Word and spend dedicated time in God's presence. Your body of knowledge about God grows, contributing to a strong foundation of truth. The more that happens, the more readily sensory data can be associated with truth. It becomes easier and quicker to recognise God's truth, because the information is not foreign to you. The more truth you possess, the less threatened you will feel when God reveals a new truth to you.

You also get to know the parts of you where chaos and sin still reign, the parts that do not align with God's truth that are keeping you from Him and the truth, limiting you, and robbing you of the fullness He wants you to experience.

We need light and sound to discern what's going on. They enable us to pay attention more effectively and to recognise our old, ragged 'truths' for the lies they are. That gives us the opportunity to get rid of them and welcome God's truth into our hearts.

Henry's dark coat of skewed perceptions kept out light and sound. He had to take off his coat for the light to enter. Initially, Anne also wore a shawl of shame around her shoulders. Henry's coat and Anne's shame misled them. They thought it would protect them against pain, but the only thing it did was to keep out God's truth.

When Anne's heart started searching for God and her gaze fixed on Him, his light could enter, allowing her to see the havoc her rejection had wreaked. She started to recognise Juan's behaviour for what it was – unacceptable manipulation. She identified her personal space afresh. That empowered her to take back her being and to draw clear boundaries where she, Anne, started and stopped. She managed to break free from the maze of intimidation.

The wonderful simplicity of reciting Scripture out loud focuses your listening and engages both your physical ears and the ones your heart listens with. It paves the way for deeper processing that hopefully leads to changed behaviour. Listening and seeing are prerequisites for recognising.

Recognising is a prerequisite for understanding how the world really works.

Step 3: Understanding – overcoming confusion

Incoming messages that are paused for proper arrangement contribute to a growing body of information you can use to form associations. When your way of seeing and listening introduces God's light and truth, your recognition expands. The more you recognise your false beliefs and skewed perceptions – and new, incoming truths – the more your understanding increases.

> **Unless you hate sin with the same intensity as God, your heart won't turn.**

When you understand, you welcome new truths. When experiences are consolidated, i.e. when they change from short-term to long-term, they contain specific interpretations. However, when new perspective is gained, after deeper understanding has been acquired, re-consolidation occurs. A fresh look at the same experience settles into your memory bank. This can be measured by the neuroplasticity of new synaptic connections. You weave together the old and the new in a fresh, authentic way. This becomes a net of re-created beliefs, a handy receptacle for deeper understanding. As stated previously, experience that is realigned to God's truth will lead to increased wisdom. Anne's understanding of who she was in the eyes of her Creator and Saviour freed her from a negative self-image and replaced her rejection filter with a truth filter. At last, she could experience true belonging – fully redeemed and inducted into God's kingdom. This truth filled her with great peace. She had made it home.

When you understand, the tablets of your heart are overwritten. Your reality is replaced by God's truth that is engraved on your heart. Understanding goes deeper than knowledge. Understanding brings epiphanies. It falls under the banner of wisdom, because you need understanding to apply knowledge correctly. You can have loads of knowledge, but without understanding, your knowledge will only bring harm. In Chapter 1 we saw that wisdom (understanding) cannot be separated from goodness and power. When you understand the incoming information, you will pay proper attention to processing. Understanding is like a footprint in wet cement. These footprints lead somewhere – to a place where consolidation or re-consolidation can happen with a view to future growth, change and re-creation.

Step 4: Turning – change becomes visible

Imagine you have your own home on your own piece of land, your own garden with a few trees, all neatly fenced in. You also have a gate. It is closed to strangers and other people who want to enter uninvited. People who show up out of the blue are often dangerous, even though many will claim that they felt 'led' to come or that they 'sensed' that you needed their help. Chances are you need them like you need the plague, as we saw in the story of Danny, the overwhelmed pastor.

What you actually need is God's help, and the interferences by all and sundry only slow down his work in you. Sometimes you do need the help of others (e.g. Anne could have used her dad's help). The key lies in people's motivation and their respect for you as an individual. Usually, individuals first need to reach rock bottom, a place of desperation. This does not need to be the case for you. You can be driven by a strong desire to align with God's truth. That will motivate you to open yourself to his counter-intuitive input, lay down your flimsy attempts at self-protection and grant access to his truth. Until you do, you will resist change kicking and screaming, because your limited awareness and skewed understanding will tell you that, no matter how harmful the familiar is, the unknown is even worse.

Knowledge about, or awareness of, specific aspects of your being does not guarantee change. Only when God's truth is embraced and invited to touch and saturate the deepest parts of you, the necessary adjustments can be made. You will repent as soon as the promise of deliverance sinks in. You will hate sin with the same intensity as God, for if you keep ignoring or justifying your sinfulness, your heart won't turn.

Turning changes your direction. The impact is enormous, because it requires a reorientation of your inner being. Your heart's convictions need to change, and you should be prepared to risk the unknown outcomes of your choice.

> **Change can be summed up in five Rs:**
> **Renounce and Remove (your old beliefs),**
> **Release (those you need to forgive),**
> **Replace (the old beliefs with God's truth),**
> **and Repeat (as long as you live).**

A number of factors will try to hold you back from taking this new road. These include, among others, your doubts about the risks inherent in your decision, divided focus or indecision, and unclear parameters. (*Where am I allowed to go?* Add to these doubts about your personal boundaries.) Strife, especially in your inner management, will waste precious kingdom time.

If you are unsure, faltering between two opinions, it is unlikely that you will allow God's truth into your heart. Instead, you might remain stuck in values such as humanism (If it feels good, it must be right; People's needs are more important than God's truth); popularity (favour with people, status, admiration); power and control (money and success), and non-confrontation (acceptance and inclusion at all costs).

However, you can choose to turn away from these dangerous, inadequate substitutes and turn to unity with God and harmony with his truth instead. After all, that is what repentance is: to turn away from your deceptive perceptions and towards God. Your heart and his can beat as one, and you can live in peace with your neighbour. As God said through the prophet Joel: 'Turn to Me with all your heart' (Joel 2:12). He also said: 'So rend your heart, and not your garments; Return to the LORD your God' (v 13).

You will only engage in the risky business of turning once you really repent of the things that keep you from Him, abhor sin in all its forms, and gaze upon Him until a hunger for Him is awakened deep within you.

Turning is the most active of the four steps of change (becoming aware, recognising, understanding, and turning). Now you can start tackling each thought that you were able to identify during the first step (to truly see and hear). When the Father's truth reaches all the way down into your heart, you lay down lies, false perceptions, and unforgiveness as well, because you realise that they hold no power to protect or deliver you. You not only discard the old, deceptive convictions you have recognised (seen and heard). You renounce and reject them outright. Where you have been hurt by yourself or others, you have to work through the process of forgiveness. You will know you are healed when you can worship God, standing next to someone you used to blame. Only then can God's revitalising truth enjoy a permanent place in your life. Your false convictions would have given way to his truth.

Change can be summed up in five Rs: Renounce and Remove (your old beliefs), Release (those you need to forgive), Replace (the old beliefs with God's truth), and Repeat (as long as you live). Turning does not involve making a U-turn, but it does bring a change of direction. Your new path does not have turn-offs or escape routes. When you turn, it has to be for good. Not that you would want it any other way, because you are excited about the future. This is the journey on which God will reveal Himself to you and feed your heart with the bread of life. Every day.

Your behaviour is proof to you and others that you have had a change of heart in the truest sense. Your behaviour will reflect your beliefs. It always does. Change at this level changes the way your genes express themselves, as indicated by epigenesis (the study of how experiences change the functioning of your genes). You will experience change – from your outward behaviour to the deepest parts of you. The more you get to know God's heart, the more your changed heart and deeper understanding will shine through in all you do. Little by little, you will begin to bear good fruit. These new discoveries and the accompanying joy will last for eternity.

Anne takes action

Anne's experiences seriously dented her confidence in people. When she walked into my office, she was jaded and cynical. This loss of confidence had started at a young age, and it had far-reaching consequences for her relationships and decision-making. Her core belief was: 'I can't trust other people.'

Even after I had been seeing her for quite some time, she still asked: 'Why do you keep on seeing me? Is there hope for me?' She would say things like: 'I'm sure you must be fed up with me by now.'

Fortunately, that was not even remotely true. On the contrary, I found this young woman's willingness to cooperate nothing short of admirable. I looked forward to our therapy sessions.

After Anne had started developing faith in God and faith in me as a therapist, she could embark on the process of change – a major gamble for any broken person. On her journey of discovery, Anne started to identify her skewed perceptions about life. That in itself was plenty of encouragement to confront the wrong assumptions about herself, others, life, and God. Piece by piece, she swopped every illusion and lie for the truth that liberated and revitalised her.

As she progressed through the steps of change, Anne's reality was slowly replaced by her Saviour's truth. She started to gain godly perspective. New engravings were made on the tablet of her heart. The road was not without its challenges – requiring much energy and lots of patience – but Anne emerged as a much more mature person, ready to enrich her environment, consciously and sub-consciously.

Conclusion

The most important choice of your life is: Do you want to know God? If you're keen to know Him better, you have to look at Him expectantly until you truly see Him, and listen to his words until you really hear Him. Who He really is. In your world.

When you keep your senses fixed on Him, your confidence in Him grows. He is the One who makes a new life possible. Your hope is in Him.

The way you look and listen creates room for God's light and sound to fill your life. His truth is invited and welcomed, so that your brain and the rest of you can accommodate it. In so doing, your thoughts are renewed, and your truth (convictions) is replaced with his truth.

Recognising, welcoming, and applying truth are the three beats in the dance of progress. You're not dancing anxiously on eggshells like Rita in Chapter 6. You are like David who danced 'with all his might', full of exuberant joy, before the Lord (see 2 Sam 6:14).

MEDITATE A MOMENT

1. Where are you now and where would you like to be? Why?
2. Do you want to change? Why or why not?
3. Do you really want to know God?
4. Change requires hard work, patience, and perseverance. How does that statement make you feel?
5. If you know that change is imperative, you can follow these guidelines:

- *Want to* change and choose to persevere with the process until the fruit starts manifesting in your behaviour.
- Turn your eyes and your ears to your Creator and declare that you want to know Him. Not because of what you get out of it, but because of who He is. Ask Him to reveal his truth to you.
- Follow the first four steps on your journey of change. Identify typical reactions to certain triggers in your life.
- Analyse the thoughts and convictions that cause your reactions to these triggers.
- Discern, with the help of the Holy Spirit, the lies and skewed perceptions you have about yourself, other people, and God.
- Renounce the lie and reject it as your truth, ask for forgiveness for the things you are guilty of, and forgive everyone who needs forgiveness (yourself included). Forgiveness is a process, as we will learn in some detail in the next chapter.
- Replace your old convictions with God's truth. Invite the sword of his Word into the very core of your being.
- Turn to God. Keep your heart's senses fixed on Him, the One who has begun this process in you, and who will complete it.

Prayer

*Thank you, Father, that You are even more committed
to the restoration of my heart than I am.
I am beginning to see how your heart, because of your
great love, is bent on reconciliation with me.
My King, when I gaze upon You and become aware of You,
my heart's senses come alive, and I want to know You better.
Please continue to reveal your heart to me.
I want to treasure your truth deep in my heart. Every revelation
from You stirs my soul. I want the fullness of your
truth to live inside me (Ps 119:11).
I turn to You today.
Please come, Father, and rewrite my truth by your Spirit.
Help me to discern where my truth differs from your truth.
Kindle the desire in me to correct my truth every time.
Write your truth on the tablet of my heart.
I know there are things that I cling to because they give me a sense
of security. Examine my heart and help me to recognise and
understand, so that I may reach the point where I want to change
and completely adopt your truth as mine.
Unite our hearts, Father, and let the light of your Holy Spirit
teach and inform me, to the glory of your Name.
I ask this in the Name of your Son, Jesus my Saviour.
Amen.*

---

1. The research was done by the team of the Unit for Cognition and Brain Plasticity at the Bellvitge Biomedical Research Institute in Barcelona.

CHAPTER 12

MAINTENANCE

Keep your renewal going

Vines need a specific environment to sprout shoots, grow, and bear fruit. The ideal climate has long, warm summers with sufficient sunlight and a slow transition to winter. They also require soil that is neither too wet nor too dry, and that contains the right nutrients. In conditions like these, vines can grow and eventually yield their fruit.

Jesus uses the image of a vine to illustrate our relationship with Him. 'I am the vine, you are the branches,' Jesus says (see John 15:5). When our hearts are circumcised, i.e. when we are born again when we turn, we become like wild shoots that have been grafted into the vine. It saves us.

The shoot's fibres need to grow deep into the trunk of the vine if the newly grafted shoot is to 'take' and grow. In turn, the vine's fibres need to grow into the shoot to nourish and strengthen it. Structural unification takes place until the vine and shoot become a single unit that bears fruit. The vine's sustainability, however, depends on certain processes. The shoot needs to be pruned correctly and at the right times. Dead branches and wayward ones must go.

If we are branches, how does spiritual pruning work?

Jesus says in John 15:3: 'You are already trimmed because of the word I have spoken to you' (CEB). If you read the Greek source text, Jesus literally says: 'You are already clean because of the message (Greek *log-on*) which I have spoken to you.'

He encourages his disciples by telling them that his words had already worked in them and changed them. His message trimmed the barren branches so that the remaining ones can grow stronger and bear much godly fruit.

The Greek word for 'word' is *logos*. We see it in Hebrews 4:12.

> For the word [*logos*] of God *is* living and powerful, and sharper than any two-edged sword, piercing even to the division of soul and spirit, and of joints and marrow, and is a discerner of the thoughts and intents of the heart.

God's Word is always at work in us, lovingly trimming what should not be there. But it also works with divine urgency. It continues as long as we allow his light into our lives and keep our eyes fixed on Him, acknowledging our dependence (see Heb 12:1–2).

We (the branches) are made to remain in Jesus (the vine), and He in us. Ours is a posture of complete submission. If we submit to the world and its expectations (if we make that our truth), we become its slaves. If we submit to Jesus, He sets us free.

Wisdom and old age

A young friend once listened intently to a few older men discussing some profound topics around a fire. They were sincerely trying to fathom the reasons for a friend's suffering, but things somehow did not make sense. The whys and wherefores piled up while the embers were cooling down.

The list of possible causes grew ever longer, but the men were none the wiser. The young man, who was sitting nearby, grew increasingly frustrated as he listened, until he could not stand it anymore. He was done listening to the old men's incessant speculation.

'I've had enough!' he cried, jumping up. Animatedly, he shared his disillusionment with the group around the fire: Old age was not a guarantee of wisdom. He may have been the youngest among them, but he did not think the older men's words spoke of wisdom at all. He said that wisdom could only come from the life-giving breath of the Almighty that gave understanding. Do read his words in Job 32. This young man was Elihu, one of Job's friends, the one who only joined later. His words are a precious reminder to us.

Wisdom is a collective noun

Wisdom is a gift, an absolutely vital one. God gives it to anyone who asks for it, but we should not ask without due consideration. Our need for wisdom should come from the heart. James said the following:

If any of you lacks wisdom, let him ask of God, who gives to all liberally and without reproach, and it will be given to him.

– JAMES 1:5

In Job 32–37, Elihu talks to Job about God. He describes God in the most poetic terms and pleads with Job to ponder God's existence and to gaze upon Him so that he can truly see and get to know Him. Once Job does that, he will no longer be confused about his relationship with God, even in his time of sorrow.

Knowing God is wisdom. One can possess all the knowledge in the world and still not have an ounce of wisdom. You can have knowledge about God and still have no wisdom. But when you really know God, you are in a covenant relationship with Wisdom Himself.

When you are joined to the Source of life, you can apply your knowledge with wisdom. His Spirit gives you wisdom that includes knowledge, understanding, discernment, good judgement and insight.

Discernment

Paul says in 1 Corinthians 2:12: 'Now we have received, not the spirit of the world, but the Spirit who is from God, that we might know the things that have been freely given to us by God.'

Things are not always what they seem. Therefore, we need to be on our toes and alert, so that we do not fall into snares of deception. For this reason, Paul prays that the Philippians will learn to discern 'the things that are excellent' (see Phil 1:10), and that the Colossians' spiritual understanding will increase (see Col 1:9). Spiritually, you should also aspire to intelligent discernment and insight.

Jesus often warned his disciples against false prophets (see Matt 24:11) and that warning is no less applicable in our day. We often look to the church or to 'church people' for healing, but sometimes we end up more hurt than when we started. We should bear in mind that there is a world of difference between Church as an institution and Church as the living, dynamic body of Christ. The institution can, at times, be more restrictive than a python. This hurts the body of Christ and deals harsh blows to God's kingdom.

We go to church in hopes of finding a place of nurture, safety, and unconditional acceptance. Unfortunately, some church institutions do not practise this type of unconditionality. Instead, their message is one of judgement and behavioural requirements that are more man-made than God-ordained. Fortunately, there are many churches that understand Jesus's heart for his broken children and who are prepared to accompany wounded people on the road to healing.

Discernment comes from a heart judgement.

Unless you want to learn the hard way, you need discernment to figure out in which type of church you find yourself. Everything may look Christian, fine, and dandy on the surface, but do not stop observing too soon. Rather ask God for wisdom and finely tuned perception. Over time it will become easier to discern his voice.

You do sometimes find wolves in sheep's clothing in some church institutions. They look like the other members or leaders, speak the same language, and observe the same habits. It is sad that they manage to deceive so many. They leave a trail of disillusioned people in their wake. You see their confusion and hear their pleas for help. 'What is God trying to tell me?' 'Is there something wrong with me?' 'I must be worthless.' I will never be good enough for church … or for God.' If you don't beware, they will trap and manipulate you with rules and legalistic jargon that have nothing to do with the Good News.

In Ezekiel 34 we also read about leaders who abdicated their role and shunned God in their search for personal gain. God warns these leaders. The members of his flock are precious to Him. He won't stand for it if someone tries to deceive them.

So, what will become of the flock? Have they been abandoned to wicked leaders? No, not if we ask God for wisdom and remain on the lookout. We should not be naive. If we turn to Jesus, we shall see our true image reflected in his eyes. The mirror of his eyes is perfectly true. In Him we see truth. When we recognise who we are and who He made us to be, that can become our truth (see Jas 1:23–24).

When you get to know Jesus as your Shepherd, follow Him, and remain in Him, He heals your wounds. Scars may remain, but only to serve as a visible reminder of his healing on your future journey. They help you to hone your sense of discernment, often in the area where you have been hurt.

True and false images of God

Discernment does not come from sensory data, logic, or knowledge. It comes from a heart judgement. The Urim and the Thummim likely were two stones that the high priest used to seek God's will in weighty matters that concerned the people of Israel. He bore them on his breastplate, over his heart. Similarly, your heart is the place in your psyche where you should seek discernment. The connection between your heart and the Father's heart is the lane along which discernment travels. You need that connection, not only to identify wolves in sheep's clothing, but also to learn how to apply your spiritual knowledge in a way that does not hurt others like you have been hurt. It can happen so easily, even if your intentions are pure, as we saw in Chapter 1.

When you do not build your faith on a relationship with God, but get carried along by a religion that consists only of rules and regulations, you start forming a false image of God. In your efforts to fit in with your rule-bound religion, you constantly drink from the cup of self-right-eousness and self-justification. Eventually, this leaves a skewed imprint on your heart of who God is and what his Word says. Consequently, your whole Christianity flows from a poisoned well. Unwittingly, you do enormous damage to yourself, other believers, and also potential believers. Living under such an impression will leave you unable to taste the difference between God's living water and the bitter dregs of stale religion. The person in such a state does not even realise the magnitude of their need for God's truth! Divine intervention is sorely needed.

Discretion

Godly discretion enables you to observe people and situations with wisdom, and to make wise choices about your behaviour towards them. Because you give due consideration, your involvement makes the person or situation better. What you see and hear is streamed to your brain, which uses the data to determine and support your immediate response. When my husband walks in the door after a tough day of meetings and demands, I should be perceptive and judicious enough to realise that there are better opportunities to complain about the stove that gave up the ghost and the children who are at each other's throats. Discretion and wisdom will help you to spot your teenager's sadness and not to make additional demands on her. At work, it will help you to 'read' your clients and colleagues so that opportunities do not go to waste.

If you lack such sensitivity, you are like church members who ring up the pastor after the service to tell him about the things he should have mentioned in his sermon. They do not care that it is lunchtime, but expect the pastor to drop everything and give them his undivided attention. Then there are the church members who believe that they have the gift of prophecy and who consider it their sworn duty to provide 'guidance' to the pastor about his leadership or personal life. Remember Danny?

If the Word is not communicated in the right way and at the right time, it could lose its impact. Everyone who follows Jesus, needs wisdom and discernment to focus on the really important things. The author of Proverbs has much to say about wisdom. He encourages the young man to whom he writes to seek it out:

> When wisdom enters your heart,
> And knowledge is pleasant to your soul,
> Discretion will preserve you;
> Understanding will keep you.
>
> – PROVERBS 2:10–11

He also says:

> A word fitly spoken is *like* apples of gold
> In settings of silver.
>
> – PROVERBS 25:11

Due consideration (discretion) and discernment have much to do with divine timing. We should entrust our words to the Holy Spirit and wait on Him to show us the correct way and time to act.

Wisdom and the Holy Spirit

In Proverbs 8, it is Wisdom personified's time to speak. The Lord had brought her forth as the first of his works, when He began his work.

> For wisdom *is* better than rubies,
> And all the things one may desire cannot be compared with her.
> 'I, wisdom, dwell with prudence,
> And find out knowledge *and* discretion …
> 'The Lord possessed me at the beginning of His way,

Before His works of old.
I have been established from everlasting,
From the beginning, before there was ever an earth …
For whoever finds me finds life,
And obtains favour from the LORD.

— PROVERBS 8:11–12, 22–23, 35

You may be smart in other people's eyes, but that does not make you wise. Also, your knowledge does not guarantee that you will receive wisdom. You only receive wisdom when you accept the invitation to Wisdom's table.

'Come, eat of my bread
And drink of the wine I have mixed.
Forsake foolishness and live,
And go in the way of understanding.'

— PROVERBS 9:5–6

If you respond to this invitation, Wisdom will make you her protégé. In Isaiah 11:2 we read:

The Spirit of the LORD shall rest upon Him,
The Spirit of wisdom and understanding,
The Spirit of counsel and might,
The Spirit of knowledge and of the fear of the LORD.

What happens when you say 'yes' to wisdom? When you turn to God and respond to his call, the elements of your inner being click into place. You become realigned and start moving in the position for which you were created: to be reconciled to God. When you are willing to do this and respond to God's invite, your gaze turns towards Him. You seek Him out, because you want to know Him.

Jesus, the Son of God, perfectly finished his assignment on the cross. There He conquered sin and death. After his resurrection, He took up his position of honour next to the Father. Then the Holy Spirit came and introduced us to Him and to the impact that his blood, the blood of the Lamb, makes in our lives. Every time the Spirit reveals Jesus to us, He teaches us what wisdom is. Jesus is the very embodiment of godly wisdom (see 1 Cor 1:24, 30)

However, you have to invite Him in and trust Him. Sometimes we can only manage it moment by moment, day by day, but we should do it until it becomes as natural as breathing.

Trust stretches capacity

In Chapter 1, we talked about the divine threefold cord: wisdom, power, and goodness. It forms part of the definition of faith. You do not truly believe before you trust these three attributes of God with your whole being.

> **Trauma can damage or
> even destroy your
> ability to trust.**

Faith stems from the discovery of who God is. Trust, however, comes from the relationship you have with your Father and your Saviour through the Spirit's revelations. Trust is faith that has been nurtured in a relationship.

Trauma can damage or even destroy your ability to trust. When we are threatened, we often promise ourselves things. Those promises then become iron-clad contracts between our heart and our will. We say things such as: 'I will never again allow others to bully me. I will look out for myself. Nobody is really safe.' One of Michael's inner promises (Chapter 1) was: 'From now on I will live in such a way that God will never again be disappointed in me. He will see that I am pure after all.' However, it is impossible to keep these promises. When you commit yourself (knowingly or unknowingly) to these promises, they become like prison guards that police your choices and behaviour. Disappointment is bound to follow and, inevitably, it does.

> **Trust is a catalyst for light,
> input, and influence.**

Sometimes you have a deep conviction that you must look after yourself 'because nobody else will'. The reason for this is that you do not trust anybody else – neither God nor people – to do it. Anne had that problem. Mistrust is a defence mechanism, but not a very effective one and it only leads to disillusionment. You were not created to protect yourself against the way life unfolds. Your responsibility to protect yourself stops at aspects that are, humanly speaking, under your control. (We saw as much in Chapter 5.)

When you trust another person, you open yourself up, stop clinging to harmful forms of self-protection, and make yourself vulnerable. You grant that person access to your inner being. When you open yourself up to the living God, you can rest assured that He does not take your invitation lightly.

The Creator God is both light and truth. In his light, truth shines. Trust is a catalyst for light, input, and influence. Your trust in Him gets this process going. God's light makes recognising possible, and recognising leads to sustainable change. Trust opens doors you did not know you had and makes change possible. When you embrace this change, you give permission for a chemical change (in your DNA), a spiritual change, and a heart change as well. When a new concept penetrates all the way to heart level, change becomes long-term. If change is founded on God's truth, the imprint should last forever.

Trust arranges all the aspects of your being in their proper position and rank so that you can have an impact on your environment. *The Amplified Bible* defines faith in Christ Jesus as follows:

> The leaning of your entire human personality on Him in absolute trust and confidence in His power, wisdom, and goodness
> – COLOSSIANS 1:4

When you believe, you lean on God with your entire being, all your energy, and your total personality. It is the sure knowledge (see Heb 11:1) that He is trustworthy and that you are completely safe with Him.

If a worldwide pandemic strikes, everyone is expected to adapt. And adapt some more. Again. And again. The incessant pressure to adapt places our inner beings under pressure. Every person has a certain level of resilience – the ability to adapt and bounce back after adversity.

As your trust increases in the One in whom everything holds together (Col 1:17), so your ability to adapt will also increase. Global changes are sure to test your resilience. It is as good an opportunity as any to grow your trust in your Father, the One who prepared eternity for you. He is firmly in control!

Intellectual assent is not enough. Many people believe that way, and so do the demons (see Jas 2:19). Belief that is built on trust is cultivated and flourishes in a personal, intimate relationship with God. When you choose to trust, you file a motion of confidence in the power of relationships. Trust creates a safe haven for you, a place of rest. It enables you to surrender to God and to submit yourself to Him. Home at last.

Your relationship with yourself

The relationships you have with others mirror your relationship with yourself. Self-acceptance and self-respect form part of the message that you have a right to be here because God created you and loves you. Love for others should be an extension of the love you have for yourself. This implies that you will only be an effective ambassador for God's good news when you understand and embrace his unconditional love for you. Love for self should not be confused with self-obsession. Healthy self-love is a celebration of the gift of life and the grace to enjoy its highs and persevere through its lows.

It is easy to find out whether your relationship with yourself is dominated by love or fear – just listen to your inner conversation. How do you talk to yourself, and what do you say when you talk to others about yourself? You should pay close attention to the language of your heart. Your heart language reveals your secrets: self-rejection, self-pity, bitterness, jealousy, fear, and self-centredness. Fortunately, it also reveals your dreams and motivation, your ideals, and your hunger for God.

To get rid of your negative truths (convictions) and change your inner dialogue, sometimes you have to embark on a journey of self-forgiveness.

Forgiveness – two sides of the coin

Regardless of how long and how intently you focus on your past, nothing will get better without forgiveness. In fact, you are bound to descend to the depths of despair without it. Do you remember William's story in Chapter 2?

> **Forgiveness is one of the big hurdles on the road to healing.**

Forgiveness does not mean pretending that someone else's sin or your own never happened. Neither does it mean that you have to downplay its impact. In fact, to see exactly how sin deceived and poisoned you, you need to honestly examine, recognise, and understand it. That is a good opportunity to address the hurt you have suffered – after you have separated it from the person who hurt you.

Then you choose – without emotion or logic – to banish the effect of this sin from every part of your being. When you stand in the circle of forgiveness, it is almost always possible to consider both types of trauma. (See Chapter 5 for a detailed explanation.)

When you want to unpack trauma properly, you have to pay attention to both sides of the coin. For example, when Anne lists the things she has to forgive her dad for, she needs to consider both the things he did and the things he failed to do. 'I forgive my dad *for* making me feel emotionally unsafe.' And: 'I forgive my dad *for not* building a father-daughter relationship with me.'

When you forgive, you have to consider the things that were done to you, as well as essential things that were left undone or not followed through.

When you separate the sin from the person who perpetrated it, it becomes easier to clearly focus on the sin that needs to be handled. It is important to note here that Anne's dad never once in her childhood consciously intended to neglect her. He is therefore unaware of the resentment she carries towards him. To her, however, he was not the dad she had needed, and that is what she has to forgive him for. Anne has to respect her dad as the man who was appointed over her as her parent, while working through his negative behaviour (as perceived by her). She has to forgive him for rejecting her, even if that rejection is *her subjective experience*.

Forgiveness is one of the big hurdles on the road to healing, especially when it comes to self-forgiveness and the acceptance of God's forgiveness. Unfortunately, self-flagellation is quite popular on many people's to-do lists. They struggle to believe that they are eligible to experience joy. Somehow, they feel unworthy of it. Just like Michael in Chapter 1, they lock themselves in a jail of conditional acceptance. This sabotages their journey to peace and wholeness. You need to apply the principles of forgiveness to yourself before you can make any headway on the journey of healing.

More often than we'd like to admit, we have to 'forgive' God as well. We often have flights of fancy about things God ought to do for us, things that are neither Scriptural nor good for us. When these things do not materialise, we are disappointed in God and feel let down by Him.

Forgiveness is a vital key in your ability to move on towards change and wholeness.

The two legs of forgiveness

If you do not follow the process of forgiveness to the very end, your wounded heart will come back every so often to make life miserable. Judgement that stems from unforgiveness clouds godly discernment. It is a potent poison. Only a drop is needed to re-infect an old wound. A comprehensive detox requires close self-examination – turning your gaze towards yourself.

Complete forgiveness stands on two legs.

1. You must forgive the person who wronged you (remember both aspects, i.e. things they did and essential things they failed to do).
2. You must ask forgiveness for any resentment and judgement you harboured towards the person.

If you do the former but neglect the latter due to pride, you will not taste the sweet fruit of forgiveness. Improperly handled forgiveness will hinder your progress and tempt you to try alternative ways of making life meaningful.

Your forgiveness does not absolve other people of their sin. However, it should make them more receptive to the gentle work of God's Spirit to convict them of sin (where applicable). Thus, the eternal work God is doing in your heart might be extended to someone else's.

When your decision to forgive reaches your heart and prompts it into action, the heavy doors to your past are unlocked. The King of kings then enters your past. After all, He is not bound by time. He will gently take the scattered bits of your heart, heal them with his love, and re-attach them where they ought to be.

Why do you still hesitate to forgive? Why do you struggle for years before letting go? Are you waiting for the guilty party to come begging for forgiveness in sackcloth and ashes? Do you want them to pay for what they did to you? You might wait your entire life, and then it still might not happen. Remember, your healing is conditional. It requires forgiveness for those who wronged you – yourself included.

Elsie

She grabs her daughter's arm and hurriedly guides her towards the gap behind the couch. For some reason, he never looks for them there. Why, she does not know. Probably because logic is not his strong suit.

After things settle down, Elsie and the eight-year-old Bella emerge from their hiding place and make tea as if nothing happened. Just another Saturday.

'When will this torture end, Lord?' Elsie asks tiredly. She knows it is not good for Bella, that it will complicate Bella's marriage one day, but what can she do? She and her daughter have nowhere to go. It is a blessing that Stephen stayed at the dormitory for the weekend. He would have tried to clobber his dad.

At this point, Elsie has known this life for almost eight years. After Bella was born, Stephen tried hard to protect his mom and his little sister against the house monster. Elsie enrolled him for residence against his will. Her motherly instincts wanted to give him some reprieve from the events at home. At least that's one thing I did right, Elsie thinks. Nowadays he seldom comes home. Only a few more years, then Bella can follow.

One gloomy Monday morning, Elsie walked into my consulting room. She was 73 years old. Her locked jaw and tightly pursed lips made her mood quite clear.

Her story was one of extremes. Her unstable spouse had subjected her and the children to 34 years of torture. Several times, she considered leaving him, but he manipulated her with attempted suicides until she stopped.

She was there because she wanted comfort and reassurance that she did not deserve the horrible hand life had dealt her. She wanted me to take pity on her and to confirm the image she had of herself. After her husband succumbed to natural causes, bitterness started eating away at her like an aggressive cancer. My reaction, however, was neither what she hoped for nor expected. Of course, I felt enormous compassion for her, but not because of her past.

I pitied her because she was blind. Her inability to draw a line between the things she was responsible for and the things she was not, caused her to stumble around desperately, like a blind person in a maze. She just could not see that her spouse's sin had poisoned her all the way down to heart level. *Her* heart, not her husband's. *Her* territory, not his.

His sin had penetrated her and had spawned her own. His abuse and manipulation became her bitterness and unforgiveness. She allowed her husband's lack of respect. She also failed to remove it after it messed up the arrangement of her inner world.

If you succumb to your heart's blindness, whether knowingly or unknowingly, you allow intruders that will take over the reins of your inner council before you know it.

Peace

When forgiveness cuts you loose from past hurt, peace flows back into your life and becomes your inner judge once more. Forgiveness reconstitutes your inner being so that God's peace may freely flow through it.

In the Bible, God promises to give us good things. He wants us to accept them. When you see his heart and accept his gifts, you should guard them with your life. His gifts are precious. They have eternal value.

The first gift He gives us, is his breath in our lungs. Next comes our salvation, wrapped up with eternal life. Furthermore, He loves giving his children joy, wisdom, and peace when they ask for it. All these things are a gift of grace, completely free from the Father's hand. You merely have to look after them.

Jesus made a promise:

Peace I leave with you; My [own] peace I now give and bequeath to you. Not as the world gives do I give to you. Do not let your hearts be troubled, neither let them be afraid. [Stop allowing yourselves to be agitated and disturbed; and do not permit yourselves to be fearful and intimidated and cowardly and unsettled.]
– JOHN 14:27 AMPC

You have a choice. You can either guard your peace or let someone rob you of it. Isaiah says:

You will keep *him* in perfect peace,
Whose mind *is* stayed on *You,*
Because he trusts in You.

– ISAIAH 26:3

His peace keeps you in the right place, i.e. a place of submission and dependence on the One who truly knows you and loves you. His peace guarantees security for you, more than any person – even your parents – can offer. This security enables you to fearlessly express your unique '-ness'. Peace also creates room for impact. It enables you to live your life without a constant need for acceptance or validation. You can give generously, because your worth does not depend on what people do in return.

Our peace, however, is constantly under attack. People's opinions and societal expectations challenge it all the time. So how can you (and Elsie) treasure this precious possession?

An advisor

Let's return to Derrick at the pivotal board meeting in Chapter 10.
Hugh was the only director who had refrained from any criticism so far, but now his eyes were pleading. Derrick knew exactly what Hugh was trying to tell him. Maybe he should …

He moved his chair backwards and pressed his fingers on the walnut table. After clearing his throat, he says: 'We have suggested every conceivable plan. I know you have tried your best, but now I'm going to listen to Hugh and call in additional help.'

Another director, Damien, clutched his coffee mug in one hand and glared at Derrick. On his right, one of his assistants, Boris, tapped his pen on the stack of papers and graphs in front of him. On the far side of those papers, the rejected suggestions lay, a heap of scrunched up paper. To the left of Damien sat Thelma. She was the company's head of sales, the person who built relationships with customers and suppliers. In one hand she held a rather moist tissue. Her trademark bubbly demeanour seemed a lot more subdued than usual.

Without offering the others, one of the directors ordered coffee for the umpteenth time. He was struggling to stay awake and really hungry too. He quietly hoped that the sandwiches would have less lettuce this time round. Annoyed, he took his place next to Thelma. *I wish she would not be so upset about the whole thing*, he thought to himself. Clay pushed the whole box of tissues over to Thelma.

Hugh looked at Derrick and nodded as if he was already making the necessary arrangements. This was precisely what he had hoped for. At last. The past few days had been a to-and-fro struggle with everyone around the table trying to push through their particular solution. Hugh had tried to attract their attention a few times himself.

Bill probably suffered most. He constantly tried to reconcile everybody's suggestions. In the end, Hugh thought, he only managed to completely exhaust himself. Bill now sat with his arms folded and his head tilted backwards, softly snoring.

The doubt and frustration were tangible, yet on the surface everything seemed under control. Not one of the directors was engaged with their original portfolio. Everybody was beyond tired.

Matt pitched much quicker than anyone thought he would. Even Hugh was impressed. The Advisor had arrived. Everyone could sense a change in the atmosphere.

Intruders in your inner council

Derrick's company is a metaphor for our inner council. It can teach us much about crisis situations that stem from inner mismanagement. The managing director's lack of control and direction quickly trickled down and caused chaos throughout the company. Nobody was excited about the corporate vision anymore. Working outside their portfolios exhausted everybody and left them unable to do the work for which they had been appointed.

> **A shaky self-image will allow invaders unhindered access to your inner council.**

The chaos was caused by a leader who did not understand his role and who could not lead them wisely. The resulting confusion left the company very vulnerable to outside influences – intruders and unwelcome guests who invited themselves to the boardroom table, the centre of control and input. Likewise, confusion paralyses your discernment and hinders strong leadership and control.

If you are doubtful and if you relate to yourself and others through fear, your gates are wide open to intruders. You may open the gates in the hopes that other people will make you feel better about yourself or more acceptable. Without the discernment that wisdom brings, you are bound to overlook intruder(s). The 'strange woman' of Proverbs 2:16 might sit herself down next to you and whisper sweet deceptions in your ear, the type of things you in your woundedness *want* to hear.

If we take the metaphor of Derrick's company further, we can say that Derrick represents your heart, because the heart is the managing director of your whole being (psyche and body). Each director represents a main aspect of the self: Damien is the soul. His assistants are Thelma (emotions), Boris (thought) and Bill (will). Clay represents your body.

Derrick eventually listened to Hugh and called in an external advisor (counsellor), Matt. Hugh represents your spirit and Matt is the Holy Spirit, our Counsellor.

If you look closely, you will also see a few other characters around the table. Between Thelma and Boris is Mara (bitterness). Thelma invited her after they met when Derrick found out about Lydia's deception. Mara and Damien have become close, and she has contributed to several discussions between Damien and his team about the company crisis. The twins, Phobos (fear) and Thumos (anger), sit on both sides of Derrick as if they belong there. Their presence and whispers permeate the room like a toxic cloud. They constantly remind Derrick of his 'what if' fears.

The metaphor shows how invaders take up space and mess with your inner council during decision-making – because you granted them permission. You let them. Their methods are underhanded, but effective. These invaders rob you of the gift of peace.

A self-image that is skew or shaky will allow invaders unhindered access to membership of your inner council. Invaders do not respect or enhance your inner order. On the contrary, they try to manipulate your heart time and again to relinquish its rank and role. They will persist until your heart feels so bullied and confused that it will abdicate to anyone who would like to take over.

When that happens, you're in big trouble. If fear chairs the meeting, all decisions will have only one goal: to avoid any potentially negative result. That makes you very ineffective (see Jas 1:6). Fear leads to doubt and indecision, that will infect your entire management team.

The focus of decision-making becomes avoiding rejection, failure, humiliation, or disappointment. Decisions that are based on fear limit you and wreck your quality of life.

Everyone's board of directors looks different

At Elsie's table bitterness and self-pity huddle together. They give the past (another invader) plenty of fodder. Rejection occupies the place next to Elsie's heart and deftly manipulates the managing director. All she needs to do, is to direct Elsie's attention to all the sensory data that confirms that Elsie suffered great injustice and that life is not at all fair. After all, she never asked for such a marriage and such a life!

Michael (Chapter 1) will likely have a holier-than-thou religion sitting next to his spirit at the boardroom table. Brimming with self-consciousness and judgement, he will remind Michael at every turn of the Scriptures he had memorised, just to make sure he fulfils his Christian duty. Disappointment would be sitting opposite religion. They almost always work hand in glove. The one's presence assures the other's on the board. Michael experiences enormous confusion when he reads the Word or listens to sermons. The invaders have all but clogged up his internal filter.

One of the most influential invaders on Phillip's inner council (Chapter 7) is death. It has infiltrated every single aspect of his life.

In Phoebe's case (Chapter 3) her body moved out of its designated place and tried hard to wrestle control from the rest of the self, giving out orders to everyone else.

Each of the people about whom we have read had to fire their invaders and restore their inner order with the help and guidance of the Holy Spirit. Some, like Danny with his fear of people, had to appoint an inner bouncer to forcibly remove some of the more stubborn invaders. It is the only way to bring about inner harmony, and to once more experience God's peace. That peace guards your inner alignment.

If the rest of the self submits to the heart's authority, you can be honest with yourself, driven by conviction. When there is disharmony that results in any of the other aspects usurping the heart's position, you won't be able to act from a place of integrity. You will deceive yourself and the inner struggle will exhaust you. It will render almost every aspect of your being ineffective. Decisions that are taken while inner chaos reigns lead to decreased functioning and weakened impact. If, however, you position your inner alignment judiciously and respectfully, you can make a marked impact on your environment.

Elsie takes action

In the weeks that followed, Elsie insisted on trying to convince me that life had treated her unfairly, and that she had a right to blame others and be embittered. Her husband had done great damage to her and their children. How could she forgive him for that?

Only when she opened herself to truth, the Father could start revealing it to her. Little by little He showed her how hurt had twisted the truth inside her. Growing in insight, she started discerning between her truth, which was based on her experience, and God's truth.

When the eyes and ears of Elsie's heart were opened, her senses were healed so that she could truly see and hear (recognise and understand). The potential value of each negative experience Elsie encountered could now be unlocked. Slowly but surely, she placed each one in the Father's strong, safe hands.

> When you invite God into your past, He will create something beautiful out of your painful experiences.

Eventually, Elsie was able to place her trust in her Creator, the God who re-creates us when we open our heart to Him. Every day He patiently stands at the door of our hearts, knocking. Until we open. He desires our healing even more than we do. He knows that our past hurts can work together for the good.

Conclusion

The following illustration has a special place in my heart: Each one of us wears an invisible mantle, or cloak. It is fastened on the shoulder with buttons of gold. The velvet drapes beautifully around the body and flows downward from the back, like a waterfall.

This cloak tells our story from beginning to end. Each element is depicted by fine embroidery. The cloak constantly changes as your life progresses. Trauma threads are usually black or dark shades of grey. When heavenly beings look down upon you as you struggle to make your way through life, they read your harrowing story.

The day you decide to open the gates of your inner being to God, every one of his servants in heaven rejoices. Forgiveness rushes in and flows to every corner of the past. With great force it flows uphill, defying the natural laws of time. The One who rules over time picks at the black threads and unravels them completely.

When you turn to Him and keep your eyes fixed on God's truth – as you increasingly see, recognise, and understand Him – his creative re-creation starts radiating through your cloak. He weaves with threads of gold, deep maroon, royal purple, and rich turquoise to tell a breath-taking tale of victory.

You must realise that every bit of information that is filed in your brain has potential. Do not underestimate everyday experiences, however big or small. They all form part of your story. There is beauty hidden inside every one of them. Past hurt that is locked or frozen in your heart, detracts from your quality of life. When you invite God into your life and into your past, He will create something beautiful out of your painful experiences. He cleans them, brings out their value, and uses those threads to weave a new story into your cloak. He changes the course of your life. When you turn to Him, every step you take, your whole '-ness', trumpets the newness God, your Creator, is bringing about in you. Now your cloak's story honours God.

MEDITATE A MOMENT

1. What would you rather have? Gold and silver (riches) or wisdom? Why do you say that?
2. On a scale of 1 to 10, where 1 is 'extremely low' and 10 is 'extremely high', how would you rate your trust in God? Why specifically this number?
3. Which invaders do you need to chase from your decision-making table?
4. How and when will you do that?
5. Whom do you need to forgive? Whom do you hold responsible for things that went wrong in your life? (Remember the two legs of forgiveness.)
6. What does your cloak look like? Does your cloak honour God?
7. What will you do if it does not?
8. Does the peace of God guard your inner territory?
9. What can you do if you are not experiencing his peace?

Prayer

*Wonderful and almighty Creator of the Universe, please plant
your truth in my heart. Let it germinate, grow and bear fruit
in me. Engrave your words on the deepest part of me. Replace
every lie with the living words of your truth.*

*Your Word says that, if I turn at your reproof, You will pour
out a spirit of wisdom and revelation on me, so that I may
know your Word (Prov 1:23; Eph 1:17).*

*I want to unpack my past hurts in your presence, Father. Help me
to forgive wholeheartedly. Help me to trust you more, so that my
heart's capacity for your truth may increase.*

*King of my heart, I want your truth to spread from my heart to
every part of my being, and I long for my spirit to be connected to
your Spirit in unity and reverence. I want to worship You daily in
spirit and in truth (John 4:24) until your truth becomes part of
me, so that I may think, reason and act like You. I want to be an
emotionally balanced steward of my life. I want to live in such a
way that joy is my dominant emotion, and that fear's only role is
to keep me safe. I want your truth to free up my will to focus and
to execute my choices in complete obedience to You
and your directives in my heart.*

*Father, I pray that your truth will become part of me at a cellular
level, programmed in my genetic information, and that all my
sensory data will be filtered by your truth. May every circuit in my
neural network reflect my new thoughts and convictions.*

*Lord, I want to live in complete harmony with your truth. I want
to minister to others with your wisdom. May it be like ointment
and perfume to them (Prov 20:5, 27:9, 25:11). Lead me, so that I
may eventually minister your truth and wisdom to the heart of my
environment, my country and even the nations.*

*Heal my heart, so that I can love and serve you wholeheartedly.
Renew my life and my past, so that my cloak may declare and
celebrate the story of your re-creation work in me.*

In the Name of your Son, Jesus, my Saviour.

To the glory of your Name.

Amen.

A blessing

May your body get enough rest and be healthy.
May you feel safe in your obedience and discipline.
May your soul be joyful and fit, focused and full of enthusiasm.
May your friendships prosper and bloom.
May your spirit ever be tied to your Saviour with bonds of love.
May your heart lead with wisdom, securely anchored in your
Father's dedicated love.

ADDENDUM A

Every person is born with roughly 86 billion neurons. At birth, the connections between the neurons are either limited or non-existent; they are only formed as the baby is stimulated by its new environment. The more stimulation, the more neurons are formed. Each of the 86 billion neurons in the adult brain receives, on average, 103 synapses from 103 nearby neurons. The result is an incredibly complex connection structure.

As your connections increase, information categories form automatically. In other words, you form associations with information of a similar type. The more your knowledge expands, the easier (and faster) you process incoming information, thanks to the simplification of a wide range of associations.

When you experience something, there is an influx of electrochemical impulses to your brain. Your senses serve as gatekeepers that allow the different bits of information or data in. After that, the message is carried electrochemically from one neuron to another.

The electrical charges on the inside and the outside of the neuron differ. A charge therefore runs along the membrane. When no impulse is being conducted, the charge differential between the outside and the inside is more or less -70 millivolt (mV). That is called the resting potential.

Potassium and sodium ions (K^+ and Na^+) play the primary role in determining the electrical charges along the cell membrane. They move through ion channels formed by proteins that act like gates or portals which determine whether the ions can flow in or not. This has a direct influence on the conducting of an impulse. A neuron's firing of an impulse can determine whether the next neuron's gates open or close. If sufficient stimulation is received from the other neurons, the electrical charge of the cell can increase from -70 millivolt to -55 millivolt (mV). Such a charge is sufficient to stimulate the cell to forward the message to the next neuron.

The charge on the membrane then quickly changes to +40 mV; that is called depolarisation. Repolarisation happens when the electric charge moves beyond the baseline of the resting state. At a charge of -90 mV, a state of hyperpolarisation is reached. After this, the neuron returns to its resting state (-70 mV).

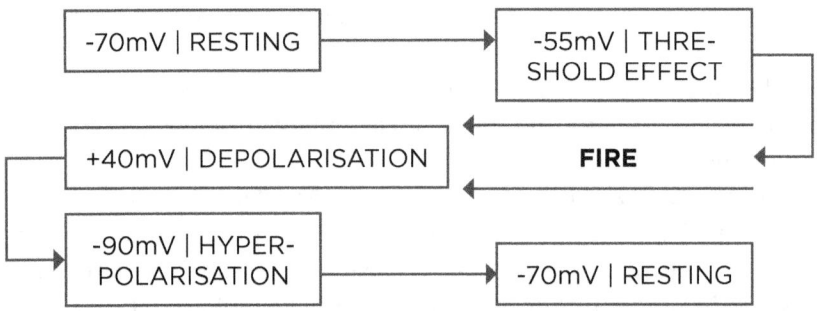

This whole cycle is called an action potential.

An action potential is produced by a branch of the neuron called the axon (see illustration on p. 166). The impulse is conducted from the axon hillock to the axon terminals. There the electric charge is converted into a chemical message. An action potential is required to transfer data from neuron to neuron. This happens in specific situations. These situations and the important role of the action potential in processing your environment were discussed in Chapter 11.

Apart from potassium and sodium, calcium (Ca^{2+}) also plays an important part in the forwarding of relevant information. One of the proteins that calcium allows through the membrane is called Orai. This protein is one of the protein portals that lets ions through. In Greek mythology, 'Orai' are the gatekeepers of heaven – making it a very suitable name for that protein. Orai plays a very important role in the processing of incoming information and, therefore, the formation of your truth. Researchers at the National Centre for Biological Science in India discovered another protein, Septin7. Septin7 acts as a guard for Orai, regulating its actions. It works as a brake on Orai's activity. When Septin7 decreases, Orai's function increases. When Septin7 is inhibited, Orai's activity increases, allowing more Ca^{2+} to go through. This leads to higher Ca^{2+} levels between cells, which can reach dangerous levels.

The misregulation of Ca^{2+} levels can lead to all kinds of problems, such as neurodegeneration (erosion) and ataxia (decrease or loss of coordination) between the spinal nerve cells and the brain.

The two aforementioned protein sentries are just another illustration of how your body selectively interacts with incoming information.

ADDENDUM B

The genetic language is very interesting. DNA has a double helix structure that consists of the following bases: adenine (A), cytosine (S), thymine (T) and guanine (G). DNA bases connect to form long molecule strings. The process of connecting is called protein biosynthesis.

It is a fascinating process that puts our Creator God's mind-boggling creativity on display. A string is divided into codons. A codon consists of three of these basis pairs. That determines how the amino acids will succeed one another. Amino acids are the building blocks of proteins. A codon can be compared to selected letters that are grouped together to form words, which build sentences when put together.

There is even a codon that acts as an indicator that the message has ended, like a full stop at the end of a sentence (see graphic on p. 224). Research that was done at Yale University's Systems Biology Institute in April 2016 shows that certain proteins (HOXA11 and FOX01) act as if they have to decide whether to execute their tasks or not. Furthermore, it seems as if these proteins' interaction can inhibit or activate genetic expression. It is an extremely important aspect to keep in mind as you go through the steps of change.

As mentioned earlier, experiences can cause changes at the DNA level. Epigenesis is the science behind the studies on how the development, functioning and adaptation of biological systems can change DNA expressions when external experiences occur. The activity and expression of your DNA composition is directly affected by your experiences.

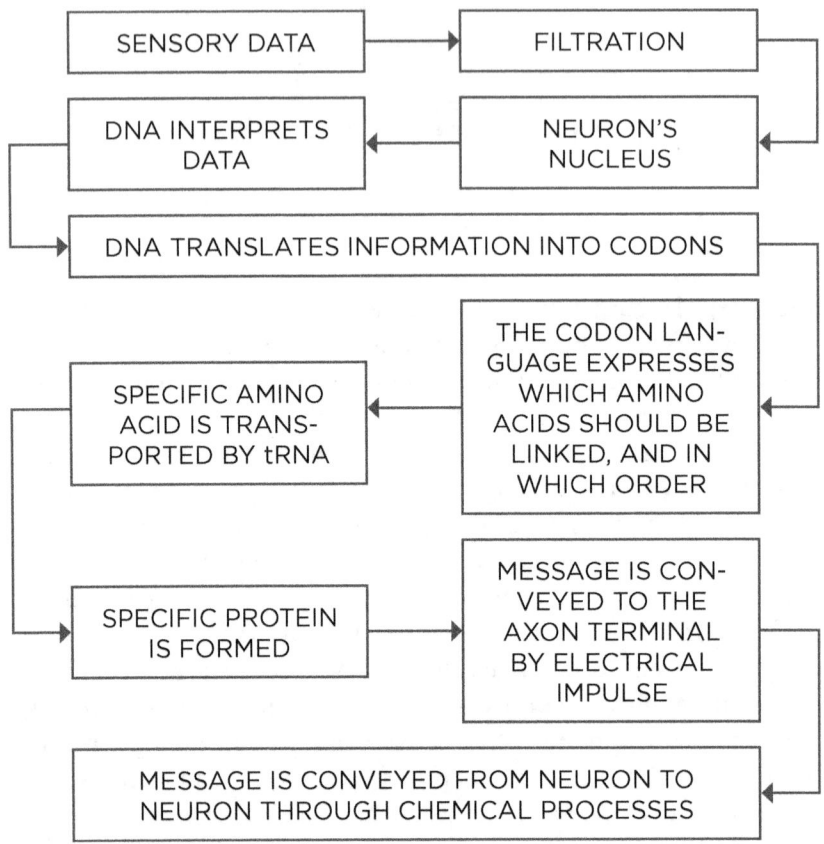

Data from outside is carried by your transfer ribonucleic acid (tRNA) via the processing path chosen by your DNA's interpretation, or DNA expression, as it is also called.

If you experience a number of similar stimuli, specific proteins will be produced. These proteins, the cell's reaction to them, and the synapse area can be affected, therefore they adapt to the incoming data. During memory formation, the DNA and RNA initiate the production of certain proteins. These proteins change the axons' connections.

During formation, it is the transfer RNA (tRNA) that carries the specific amino acid, as dictated by the codon language. These connections need to be made moments after the event to form long-term memories. Memory formation can be prevented by either blocking DNA transcribing to tRNA, or the translation (conversion) of tRNA to the specific amino acid (protein) which is necessary for effective consolidation. (Consolidation is the conversion of short-term memory to long-term memory.) To form long-term memory, the post-synaptic cell is required to produce specific proteins.

Thus, information is carried over the synapse area and from neuron to neuron by chemical processing. Neurotransmitters serve as vehicles to carry the electrochemical impulses from axon to axon. The more corresponding messages there are, the more stimulation there is from specific receptors. The concentration of receptors increases with stimulation. The receptors, in turn, look for further stimulation.

Receptors are like locks that need to be opened by keys, in this case neurotransmitters.

The nervous system can generally be divided into three functional units: sensory, motor, and association units. External stimuli, such as data that makes it past our senses, are processed as neural impulses, which paint an inner picture of a person's external reality. The association unit groups this sensory data with similar information bundles that the new information can easily associate with. In other words, this unit handles the integration of sensory data with associations of emotion and conviction. These associations, in turn, lead to motor behaviour. The motor unit enables a person to manipulate their environment by influencing their own and others' behaviour through actions and communication.

BIBLIOGRAPHY

Axline, V.M. 1993. *Play Therapy*. 33rd edition. Haughton: First Ballantine Books.

Banich, M.T. 2004. *Cognitive Neuroscience and Neuropsychology*. 2nd edition. Boston: Houghton Mifflin.

Baron, R.A. & Byrne, D. 2000. *Social Psychology*. 9th edition. Boston: Allyn and Bacon.

Basbaum, A.I. & Julius, D. 2006. Toward Better Pain Control. In: *Scientific American*. June:5057.

Bayshaw, J. & Fox, I. 2005. *Baby Massage for Dummies*. Indianapolis: Wiley.

Beauregard, M. & O'Leary, D. 2007. *The Spiritual Brain. A Neuroscientist's Case for the Existence of the Soul*. New York: HarperCollins.

Beck, A.T. & Weishaar, M. 1989. Cognitive Therapy, in A. Freeman, K.M. Simon, L.E. Beurler & H. Arkowitz (ed.). *Comprehensive Handbook of Cognitive Therapy*. New York: Plenit. 2136.

Betley, J.N., Xu, S., Cao, Z.F.H., Gong, R., Magnus, C.J., Yu, Y. & Sternson, S.M. 2015. Neurons for Hunger and Thirst Transmit a Negative Valence Teaching Signal. *Nature*, 521(7551):180185. DOI:10.1038/nature14416.

Burk, A. 2014. *The Compass and the Gyroscope Part 2*. Available: http://www.thesig.com.

Buys, A. 2005. *Soul Care School*. Kanaan Ministries. Available: http://www.kanaanministries.org/Downloads/SCS/SCSBK107.pdf

Cacabelos, R. 2017. Journal of Clinical Epigenetics. Neuroepigenetics: Prospects and Illusions. Institute of Medical Science and Genomic Medicine. DOI:21767/24721158.100069

Carter, R., Aldridge, S., Page, M. & Parker, S. 2009. *The Brain Book*. London: Dorling Kindersley.

Cell Press. 2016. A Single Species of Gut Bacteria Can Reverse Autism-related Social Behavior in Mice. *ScienceDaily*. 16 June. Available: www.sciencedaily.com/releases/2016/06/160616140723.htm.

Colman, A.M. 2006. *Oxford Dictionary of Psychology*. 2nd edition. Oxford: Oxford University Press.

Deb, B.K., Pathak, T. & Hasan, G. 2016. Storeindependent Modulation of Ca^{2+} Entry Through Orai of Septin7. *Nature Communications*. DOI:10.1038/ncomms11751

Dahlitz, M. 2017. *The Psychotherapist's Essential Guide to the Brain*. Brisbane, Australia.

De Sousa, R. 2003. Emotions and the Topography of the Mind. In E.N. Zalta (ed). *Stanford Encyclopaedia of Philosophy*. Available: https://plato.stanford.edu/entries/emotion/#toc.

Duke University. 2016. Window Into the 'Gut's Brain': Realtime View of Enteric Nervous System Provides New Way to Study Gastrointestinal Disorders. *ScienceDaily*. 7 June. Available: www.sciencedaily.com/releas es/2016/06/160607080342.htm

Duman, R. 2002. *PTSD and the Brain: What's New in Basic Research*. Western Haven: Laboratory of Molecular Pathogenisis and Treatment Mechanisms within the Clinical Neurosciences Division of the National Centre of PTSD.

Fitzgerald, M.J.T. & Folan-Curran, J. 2002. *Clinical Neuroanatomy and Related Neuroscience*. 4th edition. San Diego: Harcourt.

Friesen, J.G., Wilder, E.J., Bierling, A.M., Koepcke, R. & Poole, M. 1999. *Living from the Heart Jesus Gave You: The Essentials of Christian Living*. East Peoria: Shepherd's House.

Friesen, J.G. 1992. *More than Survivors*. San Bernardino: Here's Life.

Gamon, D. & Bragdon, A.D. 2002. *Learn Faster and Remember More*. South Yarmouth MA: Allen D Bragdon Publishers.

Gitt, W. 2003. *Fassinerende Mens*. 1st edition. Bieleveld: Christeliche LiteraturVerbreitung.

Goleman, D. 2006. *Social Intelligence*. London: Hutchinson.

Gribbin, J. 1998. *Q is for Quantum, Particle Physics from A to Z*. London: Phoenix Giant.

Herd, A. 2009. Why a Broken Heart Really Does Hurt. In: *Proceedings of the National Academy of Sciences*. Oakland: University of California. 18 August.

Hong, S., Negrello, M., Junker, M., Smilgin, A., Their, P. & De Schutter, E. 2016. The Eyes are the Window to the Brain. *Neuroscience News*. DOI:10.7554/eLife.13810.

Janov, A. 1991. *The New Primal Scream*. London: Little, Brown.

Jawer, M. 2014. The Spiritual Anatomy of Emotion. University of Virginia's School of Medicine. *Psychology Today*. August 2014.

Kahneman, D. 2011. *Thinking, Fast and Slow*. London: Penguin Books.

Kaplan, H.I. & Sadock, B.J. 1994. *Synopsis of Psychiatry*. 8th edition. Philadelphia: Lippincott, Williams & Wilkins.

Karb, S., Malsert, J., Strathearn, L., Vuilleumier, P. & Niederthal, P. 2016. Sniff and Mimic: Intranasal Oxytocin Increases Facial Mimicry in a Sample of Men. *Hormones and Behavior*. DOI:10.1016/j.yhbeh.2016.06.003

Kong, D., Dagon, Y., Campbell, J.N., Guo, Y., Yang, Z., Yi, X., Aryal, P., Wellenstein, K., Kahn, B.B., Sabatini, B.L. & Lowell, B.B. 2016. A Postsynaptic AMPK→p21Activated Kinase Pathway Drives Fasting-induced Synaptic Plasticity in AgRP Neurons. DOI:10.1016/j.neuron.2016.05.025

Korb, A. 2011. Prefrontal Nudity: The brain exposed. *Psychology Today*. 17 November. Available: https://www.psychologytoday.com/blog/prefrontal nudity.

Le Doux, J. 2004. *The Emotional Brain*. London: Orion House.

Le Roux, R. & De Klerk, R. 2003. *Emosionele intelligensie*. 3rd edition. Cape Town: Human & Rousseau.

Leskovec, J. & Horvitz, E. 2007. Planetaryscale Views on an Instantmessaging Network. In: *Microsoft Research Technical Report MSR-TR-2006-186*. June.

Louw, D.A., Van Ede, D.M. & Louw, A.E. 1998. *Menslike ontwikkeling*. 3rd edition. Pretoria: Kagiso.

McClay, R. 1996. *The Pineal Gland, LSD and Serotonin*. Available: http://www.serendipity.li/mcclay/pineal.html.

McCraty, R., Atkinson, M. & Tomasino, D. 2003. *Modulation of DNA Conformation by Heart-focused Intention*. HeartMath Research Center, Institute of HeartMath, Publication No. 03008. Boulder Creek, CA. Available: http://www.aipro.info/drive/File/224.pdf

Murphy, K. 2020. *You're not Listening*. Penguin, Random House, U.K.

Murray, A. 1944. *Die ware wynstok*. 1st edition. Brakpan: Verenigde Gereformeerde Uitgewers.

NYU Langone Medical Center. 2016. Mice on Wheels Show How Exercise Benefits the Brain. *Neuroscience News*. 2 June. Available: http://neurosciencenews.com/bdnfexerciseneuroscience4362/

Oyarzun, J.P., Packard, P.A., DiegoBalaquar, R. & Fuentemilla, L. 2016. Motivated Encoding Selectively Promotes Memory for Future Inconsequential Semantically related Events. *IDIBELL*. DOI:10.1016/j.nlm.2016.05.005

Poutahidis, T., Kearney, S.M., Levkovich, T., Qi, P., Varian, J.B., Lakritz, J.R., Ibrahim, Y.M., Chatcigiagkos, A., Ailm, E.J., & Erdman, S.E. 2013. Microbial Symbionts Accelerate Wound healing via the Neuropeptide Hormone Oxytocin. DOI:10.1371/journal.pone.0078898

Rockefeller University Press. 2016. Mobilizing Mitochondria May Be Key to Regenerating Damaged Neurons: Mouse Study. *Neuroscience News*. 7 June. Available: http://neurosciencenews.com/mitochonridaneurogenesis4397/

Rudd, S. *East Orientation of Jewish Temples and Altars*. Available: http://www.bible.ca/archeology/biblearcheologyjerusalemtemplemounteastorientationjewishtemplesaltars.htm [11 Augustus 2016].

Smith, D. 2008. Proof! Just Six Degrees of Separation Between Us. *The Guardian*. 3 August. Available: www.theguardian.com/technology/2008/aug/03/internet.email.

Strong, J.H. 1987. *The Exhaustive Concordance of the Bible*. Ada MI: Baker Books.

Van der Watt, J., Barkhuizen, J. & Du Toit, H. 2012. *Interliniêre Bybel Grieks-Afrikaans Nuwe Testament*. Vereeniging: CUM.

Ward, J. 2009. *The Student's Guide to Cognitive Neuroscience*. New York: Psychology Press.

Williams, E., Chang, R.B., Strolic, D.E., Umars, B.D., Lowell, B.B. & Liberles, S.D. 2016. Sensory Neurons that Detect Stretch and Nutrients in the Digestive System. *Neuroscience News*. DOI: 10.1016/j.cell.2016.05.011

Yale. 2016. In Genetic Decision Making, Proteins Learn to Listen to Each Other. *Neuroscience News*. 29 Mei. Available: http://neurosciencenews.com/geneticsproteinsdecision4340/

ABOUT THE AUTHOR

Gerdi van den Berg has been involved in pastoral counselling and cognitive behavioural therapy for more than 25 years. Her passion is to support people on their road to healing. She believes that people consist of a body and spirit, with the spiritual heart as the core. These aspects of our being function interdependently. Before you understand, acknowledge, and repair the role each part plays, you will not be able to function effectively as a person.

Gerdi obtained a B.Sc. degree in Biochemistry at Free State University, an Honours degree in Psychology at the University of Stellenbosch, and a Masters' and Doctorate in Sociology (in the socio-cognitive field) at Trinity University in Delaware in the United States. During her studies, her research centred on socio-cognitive neuroscience, focusing on the social and motivational aspects of human behaviour, information processing and decision-making, as well as the various brain mechanisms involved in these processes.

She has authored a book on the impact of trauma on the spiritual journey, a manual for counsellors who focus on dissociative identity disorder, course material about neuroscience for students at the Institute for Christian Psychology, and course content on self-assertiveness for students at a hotel school.

For ten years, Gerdi formed part of an international ministry organisation and regularly travelled to countries like Germany, Austria, and Taiwan. During and between conferences, she offered spiritual counselling to attendees.

At the moment, she runs her own counselling practice where she offers pastoral counselling and cognitive behavioural therapy, both in-person and online. Gerdi and her husband, Cobus, have been married for 33 years. They have three children, two of whom are married, and one grandchild.

HEART MATTERS COUNSELLING AND TRAINING

For more information about counselling and training offered by Heart Matters, scan the QR code above or visit www.heartmatters.co.za